Praise

At last, a book that sees emotions as a gift from God rather than a tool of Satan. Love, sorrow, joy, fear, disappointment, excitement, frustration, and discouragement are all human emotions that can motivate us to godly living. Understanding emotions and how to process them is a major lesson in life. In *Joy and Tears*, Dr. Gerald Peterman gives practical biblical insights to help us make the most of God's gift of emotions. I highly recommend it.

GARY CHAPMAN
Author of *The 5 Love Languages*

A "word in season" unexpectedly transformed Dr. Peterman's understanding of emotions. Now in this excellent and highly practical book, he shows the way forward for God's people in this often neglected but important area of Christian living. I was surprised at how much material has been unearthed in this treasure of teaching, which includes thoughtful questions for reflection and discussion.

BRUCE WINTER
Former Warden of Tyndale House,
Cambridge (1987–2006)

There aren't many Christian books on the emotions. And there are fewer that I find myself in substantial agreement with! Thankfully, this is an area of biblical teaching that is receiving renewed interest and more faithful biblical exposition. Gerald Peterman's *Joy and Tears* should be enthusiastically added to that small but growing list. Although Peterman is an academic, and his book is indeed filled with Scripture, this is an accessible and applicable treatment of emotions in the Christian life. One might not always embrace all of his conclusions, but it is certainly a book that challenges, instructs, and edifies. The Questions for Discussion make it an excellent resource for small groups. I joyfully recommend this book.

BRIAN BORGMAN
Pastor of Grace Community Church, Minden, Nevada
Author of *Feelings and Faith*

Joy and Tears is a book I wish I would have read many years ago. Using astute theology, personal lessons, and practical advice, Peterman is an excellent tour guide over terrain that has broken many people and left others too confused to go on. Whether the issue is anger or tears, it's refreshing to find an author who welcomes us as fellow pilgrims not projects. I heartily recommend this book as a new dialogue partner to deepen your understanding of human relationships and love for our Redeemer.

ANDREW J. SCHMUTZER
Professor of Biblical Studies, Moody Bible Institute
Author of *The Long Journey Home: Understanding and Ministering to the Sexually Abused*

Joy and Tears is a must-read primer for anyone exploring the vast frontier of emotions and their impact on our lives as to how we see God, ourselves, and others. Dr. Peterman guides us to understand how rich our lives can be as we allow ourselves to feel and process emotion from God's perspective. For those just beginning to embark on the journey of understanding themselves and their emotions, *Joy and Tears* is a solid next step.

NANCY KANE
Associate Professor, Moody Bible Institute
Coauthor with her husband, Ray, of *From Fear to Love*

With scholarly insight and sincere compassion, Dr. Peterman makes a convincing case for understanding the source and meaning of our emotions as Christians. He explains through clear examples with solid scriptural evidence how our emotions can provide a deeper insight into our faith as well as give us a greater ability to share the gospel. His illuminating discussion includes practical steps on how to apply a greater understanding of feelings as expressed in Scripture and experienced by the believer. This book will be a valuable resource to every Christian who seeks an authentic and personal walk with Christ.

STEVEN R. MERSHON
Instructor, Psychiatry and Behavioral Sciences
Feinberg School of Medicine, Northwestern University

JOY AND TEARS

The Emotional Life of the Christian

Gerald Peterman

MOODY PUBLISHERS

CHICAGO

All Scripture quotations, unless otherwise indicated, are taken from The *Holy Bible, English Standard Version.* Copyright © 2000; 2001 by Crossway Bibles, a division of Good News Publishers. Used by permission. All rights reserved.

Scripture quotations marked CEV are taken from the *Contemporary English Version.* Copyright © 1991, 1992, 1995 by American Bible Society. Used by permission.

Scripture quotations marked NIV are taken from the *Holy Bible, New International Version®.* NIV®. Copyright © 1973, 1978, 1984 by Biblica, Inc.™ Used by permission of Zondervan. All rights reserved. worldwide.www. zondervan.com

Edited by Jim Vincent
Interior Design: Ragont Design
Cover Design: Faceout Studio
Cover Image: Veer / 2201167

Library of Congress Cataloging-in-Publication Data

Peterman, Gerald W.
   Joy and tears : the emotional life of the Christian / Gerald Peterman.
      p. cm
   Includes bibliographical references.
   ISBN 978-0-8024-0588-3
   1. Emotions—Religious aspects--Christianity. 2. Christian life. I. Title.

BV4597.3.P46 2013
248.4—dc23

2012043767

We hope you enjoy this book from Moody Publishers. Our goal is to provide high-quality, thought-provoking books and products that connect truth to your real needs and challenges. For more information on other books and products written and produced from a biblical perspective, go to www.moodypublishers .com or write to:

Moody Publishers
820 N. LaSalle Boulevard
Chicago, IL 60610

1 3 5 7 9 10 8 6 4 2

Printed in the United States of America

To Bethany and Grace,

from whom I have learned

and continue to learn much

Contents

1 ♦ Why Talk about the Emotional Life of a Christian?

I AM A RECOVERING STOIC. In high school one teacher commented, "Gerry, you are the most even-keeled student I have ever seen." Even-keeled was his nice word for talking about how I was emotionally distant, flat, and hard to read.

I prided myself on being consistent, and that meant having a "stable" emotional life . . . so I thought. I believed that too much of any emotion was bad, and anything more than a tiny bit was too much. *Life is about thinking and doing,* I told myself. *Besides, emotional swings are unhelpful. They're also irrational and belong to weak people.* I figured emotions did not help me with schoolwork, and they did not help me win arguments with people—only the rational helped me with that.

Of course, like everyone else I had emotions—but I wasn't able to admit that. I was in big-time denial. Whenever I recognized a strong feeling, I'd blame it on other people.

How did this happen—denying my feelings, and blaming people when I sensed emotions welling on the inside? I wasn't born a stoic baby, never crying. For me, the desire to hold in my emotions came from messages I received. When growing up I was reprimanded many times by my grandmother for any sort of negative emotion: sadness, fear, and especially anger. Being denied these normal expressions on one end of the emotional spectrum, it was the natural outcome that emotions on the other end would be tempered too. So no feelings of gladness, love. What was the result? We had someone who was seemingly "even-keeled."

I WAS CONVINCED the Christian life
was wholly about thinking. Feelings
had nothing to do with it.

There was little change after becoming a Christian in college, except that now I was able to read certain passages in the Bible as if they confirmed my previous non-Christian ideas about emotion. The discipleship group I was in, and all the sermons I heard confirmed my false opinion that Christian life was wholly about thinking (that is, believing certain things) and learning to do certain things (such as developing good stewardship habits). Feelings had nothing to do with it.

Although the Bible also speaks about learning to hate evil and love good (Amos 5:15), I concluded that "hate" and "love" are just ways of acting, not ways of feeling (a conclusion at times reinforced by Christian literature). Christians were supposed to rejoice (Philippians 4:6), so I concluded that sadness was sub-Christian or maybe even sinful.

My thoughts about anger were similar. Since Jesus said, "Everyone who is angry with his brother will be liable to judgment (Matthew 5:22), I took up my grandmother's crusade and reprimanded others for their anger, while pretending I had none. If someone else pointed out my anger, I could justify what I was doing by giving it an acceptable label. I'd say, "I'm not angry; I'm just frustrated."

It took decades for me to find out that this whole approach to life was truncated, shortchanged, and unlike Christ. Since then there has been a long road to recovery; and it's not over.

I suspect either you or close friends—perhaps both—have had a similar experience. Maybe you've been told your whole life, directly and indirectly, that emotions are bad, especially for a Christian, but now you want to give emotion a second try. Maybe you agree that our emotions are something we need to bring into the open, talk about, and evaluate in light of Scripture. Perhaps someone you know needs some convincing. If that's the case I'm glad to have you along. After all, that's why I'm writing this book. Here are a few reasons we should talk about Christians and emotions.

SUSPICIOUS OF EMOTION

A long-lived suspicion of emotion pervades the church, especially among fundamentalists and conservative evangelicals. Emotions are viewed as helpful at best but certainly substandard. At worst, many view emotions as misleading or even harmful. We can find a variety of examples, from the way we do evangelism, to the hymns we sing, to the way we go about making decisions.

Emotions and Evangelism. I recall sitting on a bench on the quadrangle of the University of Florida in April 1980, listening to the gospel. Although I had heard it all before, the gospel never made any sense until that morning. The next week, after I had received Christ, the man who shared the gospel with me did some follow-up. He went back to his tract to clarify something very important. Receiving eternal life is like a train, he said. The engine is the fact of God's Word, and faith is like the coal car. Feelings are the caboose—the train will run with or without the caboose, and so we should not trust our feelings. In the same way, as Christians we do not depend on feelings or emotions, but we place our faith (trust) in the trustworthiness of God and the promises of His Word.

What matters is faith, not feelings, he explained. Feelings are secondary and follow faith. We should not think that feelings are important for us to understand anything. Facts matter, not feelings: this is not much different from what I preached to myself as a non-Christian.

Now many years later, I have the convenience of literally taking a train to work four days a week. Do you ever take a good look at commuter trains? I've never even seen a caboose on the train I take to work. Pair that with the metaphor of salvation as a train and here's the implication: feelings matter so little that we can just drop them off altogether. Imagine my surprise to find out that feeling happy about being forgiven is a good thing, not a useless accessory (Psalm 32:1)!

Hymns and Emotions. As I write this chapter, Christmas has just passed, and I have memories of singing some old favorites such as "Silent Night," and "O Come All Ye Faithful." Christmas songs are some of the best with rich theology. One such is "Away in a Manger." In this classic we find that Jesus is Lord, that He hears prayer, that He comforts us, illuminated in such lyrics as "Be near me, Lord Jesus." But I engage in silent protest about some lyrics. For example, in stanza two we sing, "The cattle are lowing, the baby awakes, but little Lord Jesus no crying he makes."[1] What would motivate the writing of such words? Words that, if you've ever had a baby, you know are totally unrealistic. Babies often cry at strange or loud sounds. They fear the unexpected.

So why can't the infant boy cry in this setting? Well, if one has the view that negative emotions (fear, anger) are at best second rate, then one would naturally shy away from finding such emotions in the sinless Lord Jesus. That may be why the writer depicts the Christ child as serene in this less-than-perfect setting (the sounds of animals, probably cool temperatures). Unfortunately, any child singing this carol today will learn that crying at loud noises is inappropriate, perhaps even sinful.

Two beloved hymns also fault negative emotions. In Joseph Scriven's classic hymn of comfort, "What a Friend We Have in Jesus," stanza 2 rightly acknowledges that we have "trials and temptations" and (in stanza 3) that we are sometimes "weak and heavy laden, cumbered with a load of care."[2] Rightly also it encourages us to take these things to the Lord in prayer. But why does Mr. Scriven say that "we should never be discouraged"? What are discouraged people to do at this point? Is discouragement sinful? What if much prayer does not take away discouragement?

Another classic hymn, "It Is Well with My Soul," by Horatio Spafford, has offered many true comfort at funerals. The first stanza declares: "Whatever my lot, Thou has taught me to say, 'It is well, it is well with my soul.'"[3] Yet one wonders why it is that, whether we have peace or sorrow, God has taught us to say "It is well, it is well, with my soul." If God teaches us what to say to Him, surely one place He does this is in the Psalms, where we find the following:

> O Lord, why do you cast my soul away? Why do you hide your face from me? Afflicted and close to death from my youth up, I suffer your terrors; I am helpless. . . . You have caused my beloved and my friend to shun me; my companions have become darkness. (Psalm 88:14–15, 18)

Psalms such as 100 and 150 teach us to express joy and praise. Psalms such as 73 and 88 teach us to pour out to God our bitter feelings. Each expression has its appropriate time, but we would never know that from the hymns we sing.

We might think that modern songs and choruses fare better; and to their credit they certainly allow for the transparent sharing of positive feelings in worship. For example, the CD *America's 25*

Favorite Praise & Worship Choruses (Brentwood, 1995) contains well-known and rich tunes that I love. But not one of them acknowledges the pain of life and helps the Christian express pain and disappointment toward God. There are a few exceptions, where praise songs mention our emotional pain, but more need to do so. One example is "Blessed Be Your Name" (Thankyou Music, 2002), by Matt Redman, who acknowledges sometimes we walk the path "marked with suffering." More Christian songs need this balance and candor when it comes to expressing the struggles in our faith walk.

Decision Making and Emotions. During fourteen years of college teaching, I have often had conversation with students about their future. Here's a typical conversation with a student; I'll call him Ian:

"Dr. P, I've been thinking about what I should do after I graduate and I'm not sure."

"Ian, it sounds like you're going through a normal process. Tell me about it. What are you not sure of?"

"Well, I'm not sure what God wants me to do. I've been praying about it, but I haven't gotten any clear guidance."

"So what do you want to do?"

"I just want to make sure I'm doing God's will. I don't want to be out of God's will. If I do what I want, I might just be doing something wrong, something selfish."

"I commend your desire to follow the Lord. But Ian, have you ever stopped to think that your desires might be very helpful in deciding what you should do after graduation?"

"Well, uh . . . not really, no."

Why would we be suspicious of our desires when we are making decisions? Of course it is true that "there is a way that seems right to a man, but its end is the way to death" (Proverbs 14:12), and that we need to "abstain from the passions of the flesh, which wage war against" our soul (1 Peter 2:11). But we should not think that the only way sin has affected us is in our desires. Our thoughts have been damaged as well. So we should say that if we are going to be suspicious of our emotions, we should also be suspicious of our thinking about emotions. As disciples of Christ, we should be in the process of developing new minds and new affections. Which leads me to my next point:

WRONG THINKING ABOUT EMOTIONS: "I CAN'T HELP THE WAY I FEEL"

We also need to explore our emotions because of so many misconceptions about them. For instance, there's a common view—even if it is becoming less respected in philosophy—that emotions happen to us passively. They just come on us willy-nilly like a virus. This type of perspective is probably one of the causes behind a comment I heard in a Romans class I taught a few semesters ago. A student said, "My pastor gave a sermon and said that God never commands us to have an emotion. Emotions can't be commanded." Why draw the conclusion that emotions can't be commanded?

We'll talk more about this in the next chapter. For now, we just need to keep in mind that Scripture assumes that proper emotions are linked to proper convictions (beliefs). Likewise, improper emotions (for example, rejoicing in wrongdoing, 1 Corinthians 13:6) are based on wrong convictions (beliefs). If emotions come upon us like a virus, there is no hope for change. We can do nothing about joylessness. "I can't help it if I feel no joy," some say. Others protest, "I cannot help being short-tempered." But if these emotions are the natural response to our convictions, there is hope for change.

Even the way people talk—from conservative evangelicals,

to society at large—reflects this idea that we are passive in our emotional experiences. Men and women say they are "having" an emotion. Is this like "having cancer"? We might say something like "I got angry." Is this like "I got sick"? Certainly we do not choose to be sick.

You might hear a couple say, "We fell in love," as if it was wholly accidental—we were just going along and without making any choices we tripped over someone's else's good looks and good character. Again, we describe emotion as we sense it and then end up believing that our descriptions reflect reality.

IS LOVE AN ACTION
OR AN EMOTION?

We will have a whole chapter on love later, but for now I just point out that much thinking is going wrong here. A common opinion about love goes something like this:

"Love is not an emotion; it is action. Many married couples have this problem: they think that love is an emotion. So when romantic feelings are gone, they conclude that love is gone. But in fact, love is actually more of an attitude that works itself out in proper action. So if we have a proper attitude toward our husband, for instance, we can act toward him in a certain way (that is, we can love him), even when we have negative feelings toward him. Furthermore, Paul commanded that, 'older women . . . are to teach what is good, and so train the young women to love their husbands and children' (Titus 2:3–4). Now if love were an emotion, it could not be learned and it could not be commanded. Therefore, we see that love is not an emotion, but an action."

This falls far short of a scriptural view of love, and I will unpack it more in chapter 7. For now, let's mention two things:

First, if we say that love is only an action, it ceases to be a motivation for an action. In truth, the same action can have all sorts of motivations. We know this from personal experience. Take driving on the freeway, for example. On the freeway, I slow down so another driver can change lanes easily. Why? I might do this to avoid an accident (fearful motivation), or to make the person riding with me think I'm a safe driver (prideful motivation). On the other hand, I might do it because I know the stress of highway driving, I sympathize with the other driver, and would want someone to do the same for me (loving motivation).

Second, this view of emotion, and particularly this view of love, short-circuits maturity. We command people to love and we say that love is only a choice, only an action. But then we talk about love being very important and something we need to be deeply concerned about. What's the result? We produce people who feel guilty because they do not "love" (that is, they have failed to act a certain way), and who don't know what to do with their love (that is, their affection, compassion). They can't label their affection/compassion as "love" since they know that this affection they feel is an emotion; love is not an emotion, and so their affection is not love. How confusing!

In a very similar way, I will further assert that most of our decisions and actions are based in or take into account some sort of desire or aversion (or both). So when we tell people to make a rational decision apart from their feelings, what sometimes happens is that we are producing people who have a hard time making decisions. We will return to this in later chapters.

WHAT DO THE SCRIPTURES
SAY ABOUT EMOTION?

Why talk about emotions? Because the Scriptures talk about them. Scripture has much to say about emotion, and the Bible speaks to the topic in a variety of ways. One way it speaks is by reporting someone's emotional actions or reactions. Most of these examples are narrative. For instance, we read of Sarah's fear (Genesis 18:15), Hannah's joy (1 Samuel 2:1), Peter's grief (John 21:17), Paul's despair (2 Corinthians 1:8), and Jesus' anger (Mark 3:5).

Scripture can also require or forbid certain emotional actions or reactions. Most of these examples are in Psalms, Proverbs, in prophetic messages, and in New Testament letters. For example, we are commanded to hate evil (Psalm 97:10; Romans 12:9), to love kindness (Micah 6:8), to be "fervent in spirit" (Romans 12:11), and to put away wrath (Colossians 3:8).

Finally, Scripture uses language or ways of speaking that typically involve emotion, and there are many examples. When the psalmist writes, "My tears have been my food day and night" (Psalm 42:3), we know that this is an impassioned statement about his distress, not a logical objective statement about a liquid diet. When Paul rebukes the Corinthians (2 Corinthians 10–12), he often uses sarcasm. Sarcasm is often an indication of anger.

Especially important are the emotions of Jesus. Jesus is sinless (2 Corinthians 5:21; Hebrews 4:15, 7:26); He always does His Father's will (John 5:19, 8:29). Therefore any emotion Jesus experienced was not only a sinless experience, but a virtuous experience worthy of our imitation. We should ask what His emotional life tells us about our emotional life.

WHY IS IT DIFFICULT TO TALK ABOUT OUR FEELINGS?

Sometimes we need to do something painful and difficult. Talking about our feelings is one of these things. It's hard for at least two reasons. On the one hand, it's scary. It's scary because at times our emotions seem to come from out of nowhere and seem to be out of control, or because we don't fully understand our emotions and the unknown is often scary, or because we are afraid of doing it wrong and looking stupid. And because it is scary it is difficult.

By our avoidance and by our rise in blood pressure when the subject comes up, we betray that we are inept in the discussion. This leads into my second reason, which I have already alluded to: Many of us don't have the skill to talk about our emotions, because we have trouble accessing our emotions and trouble understanding them. So we might be "upset" about something and have symptoms such as increased heart rate, tightness in the body, and feeling hot in the face. But we can't figure out that we are angry because we have been hurt by a comment someone made a few minutes ago. Closer to home, if I ask a student, especially a male student, about how he feels I'll mostly get a cognitive answer. He can work at the level of his thoughts but has a hard time accessing and understanding emotion.

HOW EMOTION CAN AFFECT BOTH EVANGELISM AND MINISTRY

We need to talk about emotion, because, if we share the gospel, we must be concerned with motivations—both our motivations and our listeners' motivations. Professor Donald Carson treats this in a brief yet insightful article that I commend to you.[4]

Among New Testament preachers, Carson found messages that appeal to the listeners' (1) fear of death, (2) desire to be rid of guilt feelings, (3) strong sense of need, or (4) joyful response to the message of God's grace and love (among other motivations). Jesus and Paul appeal to people's emotions in various ways in order to make the gospel appealing, to make rejection of it very unappealing, or generally to urge proper response. Similarly, the prophets appealed to the people's emotions to make the messages of God both appealing and compelling.

Therefore, we see how legitimate emotional appeals can be used by God and effective ministers as a tool to aid in the spreading of the gospel. To leave emotions out cuts us off from an effective way of touching people's hearts and opening their ears to the Word of God. We will return to this subject later when we treat Romans 12:15.

EMOTIONS AND
UNDERSTANDING THE BIBLE

Many students of the Bible are unaware of this truth: Learning about human emotions can help them understand Scripture, especially narrative. What I mean is this: God has given us stories—not fantasy stories, but history. Certainly these stories give us historical facts, and these facts are important. Abraham and Sarah really did have a child in their old age; God really did work through Moses to bring Israel out of Egypt; Naomi and Ruth really did find a redeemer (Boaz) who gave them a new home. Underneath the facts of these stories are the themes of God's faithfulness, power, and compassion.

But while these stories give us valuable information and demonstrate key truth about who God is, they are also intended to engage us emotionally. Stories in every culture work this way. They show the emotions of characters (good and bad characters), and they inspire emotion in us. If we only let these stories engage our intellect, if we only look in the stories for facts, Scripture will only do half its work in us, because we are disengaged. The *affective* appeal is a way the writer gets our attention, draws us into what is happening in the story, and makes us ready to be struck by the message.

For example, when we learn that Abraham and Sarah are people with whom God is working to bless the world and then learn that they are childless, we ought to feel suspense. How is God going to work this out, since you can't bless the world with offspring if you are dead! When Naomi is widowed and loses her two sons, she is understandably discouraged. We should be too! We can and should feel her hurt and sense of loss. If we too feel her discouragement and sadness, then we are all the more ready to glory in God's great mercy toward Naomi in Ruth and Boaz and in their son, Obed (and Naomi's grandson; see Ruth 4:13–17).

Many characters are presented to us in Scripture so that we can relate to them. So in Luke 7:12, we see Jesus draw near to the gate of the town called Nain. Just then "a man who had died was being carried out, the only son of his mother, and she was a widow, and a considerable crowd from the town was with her." How sad this scene of mourning! And notice it moved Jesus to compassion (v. 13).

IN SCRIPTURE, some characters are presented to stir our admiration . . . or to stir our disdain for them.

Some characters are presented to invite identity with them. David is one of these. Some characters are presented to stir our admiration of them or to stir our disdain for them: admiration for Ruth, her confession, her sacrifice, her admiration of her mother-in-law, her hard work. On the other side, we are encouraged to develop disdain for Herod, his brutality, his selfishness.

When we are emotionally engaged, we are prepared to be confronted by God's message to us. That's what happened to King David as he listened to Nathan's parable. In 2 Samuel 11, we read that David committed adultery with Bathsheba, got her pregnant, and tried to cover the whole thing up by having Uriah, Bathsheba's husband, killed. Months later, David is approached by the prophet Nathan, who does not rebuke David directly, but rather tells a story:

> "There were two men in a certain city, the one rich and the other poor. The rich man had very many flocks and herds, but the poor man had nothing but one little ewe lamb, which he had bought. And he brought it up, and it grew up with him and with his children. It used to eat of his morsel and drink from his cup and lie in his arms, and it was like a daughter to him. Now there came a traveler to the rich man, and he was unwilling to take one of his own flock or herd to prepare for the guest who had come to him, but he took the poor man's lamb and prepared it for the man who had come to him." Then David's anger was greatly kindled against the man, and he said to Nathan, "As the Lord lives, the man who has done this deserves to die, and he shall restore the lamb fourfold, because he did this thing, and because he had no pity."
>
> Nathan said to David, "You are the man! Thus says the Lord, the God of Israel, 'I anointed you king over Israel, and I delivered you out of the hand of Saul. And I gave you your master's house and your master's wives into your arms and gave you the house of Israel and of Judah. And if this were too little, I would add to you as much more. Why have you despised the word of the

Lord, to do what is evil in his sight? You have struck down Uriah the Hittite with the sword and have taken his wife to be your wife and have killed him with the sword of the Ammonites" . . . David said to Nathan, "I have sinned against the Lord." And Nathan said to David, "The Lord also has put away your sin; you shall not die." (2 Samuel 12:1–9, 13)

Because David is moved emotionally by the story of the rich man's greed and brutality, he already has his defenses down. When the statement comes, "You are the man!" it's too late to be detached and defensive. His emotional engagement with the story has prepared him for the rebuke.

So we should ask the question, how do we read Scripture? We can all agree that if we are intellectually detached as we read, we are less likely to get the point. But it is also the case that if we are apathetic—that is, if we are emotionally detached as we read (or what I might call stoicized)—we are less likely to get the point. Further, if we are whole people, our thinking, acting, and feeling will all act in concert. Certainly the Bible calls us to not only proper understanding and proper action, but also to proper feeling.

EMOTIONS, MOTIVATION, AND GOALS

Why talk about emotions? Because emotions aid us in decision making and in the pursuit of goals. Almost every decision we make has a cognitive element and an emotive element.

Take Ian, whom we saw earlier in the chapter. He was suspicious of consulting his own desires while planning his future. While it is true we should not assume that our every desire is a good one, it is also true that we rarely pursue anything unless it holds out some positive emotional appeal. One person might pursue a certain job because she pictures it—she imagines it—as holding out hope for good feelings. She will feel good about using her gifts and skills, about accomplishing something that helps others, or even about making money. Another pursues a family because he pictures good times with the kids: taking them to the park, expressing pride at graduation, playing with grandchildren. These imagined future feelings need not be overt, on the surface, but they will be present nonetheless. So Ian might pursue, for instance, youth ministry because he thinks it is fun to organize events; because he has received lots of encouraging positive feedback when leading Bible studies for the Junior High group; and because he just enjoys spending time with teenagers. We rarely avoid anything unless we perceive it as holding a negative emotional appeal (we are afraid it will hurt us).

If we are to act, we must be motivated, and motivation is linked to emotion. Medical research shows that lack of emotion means lack of motivation.[5] Within one study, patients who had suffered damage to areas of the brain that produce emotion were prompted to perform a variety of activities, such as lengthy conversation, solving mathematical problems, and remembering details. They often did. Yet if not prompted, they would lie motionless in their hospital bed. Why is that? They had no emotion and so had no desire—no motivation—to act. As a result, although a particular patient could comprehend—at least at one level—what great wealth is and what a lifetime spent in prison is, neither one was appealing. Neither one was repulsive.

All this talk about positive emotional motivation might sound suspicious, as if knowing and obeying God is all about fun, as if discipleship involved no duty. Yet duty, although very important at times, is not a good motivator. Why? First, because even though it might look like selfless obedience to God's commands, it is rarely that. One who acts out of duty could be motivated by the desire to appear holy, or the desire to avoid looking unholy. Both of these are pharisaic motivations. Or one who acts out of duty might be motivated by the desire to avoid punishment—that is, fear is his motivation.

Second, if we have learned anything from the close relationships we have in our lives, we have learned that our friends and family don't want our duty, they want our affection. Imagine that, on their wedding anniversary, a husband meets his wife at the front door, a present in hand.

Husband: "Say, I got these flowers for you."

Wife: "Oh, honey, they're beautiful! You shouldn't have!"

Husband: "Of course I should have. It's our anniversary; it's required that I get you flowers."

What would motivate such a husband? Probably he fears her wrath if he does not do what he perceives is required (his duty). But after making such a foolish comment he will be fortunate if she does not throw the flowers in his face. The wife wants his affection (loving motivation), not his duty (fearful motivation).

JOY, TEARS, AND OTHER EMOTIONS: WHY THEY SHOULD MATTER TO US

As Christians, our emotions are a valid part of our lives. They do matter. As we noted, the church has a long-lived suspicion of emotion. Although God has made us both thinking and feeling creatures, we embrace the former and are nervous with the latter.

Why should we now consider our emotions? We have looked at six reasons for doing so (and, really six reasons you should read this book). First, there is much misunderstanding about how we should regard our emotions. At least one of these wrong ideas is the assertion that love is not a feeling, only an action. Second, if

Scripture has a lot to say about emotion—and it does—we should be glad to learn what it says. Third, emotion is a difficult topic for us to discuss. If we are afraid of the discussion, then we already see we have needs in this area! Fourth, if we share the gospel we must be concerned with motivation—both our motivations for sharing it and the listener's motivation to receive it. And motives are often stirred by our emotions.

The final two reasons have to do with our interest in God's Word and our personal future. Fifth, to learn the most from the Bible, we need to engage it both cognitively *and* emotionally. We understand the Scriptures more clearly and fully when our emotions are involved in the stories and applications of the Bible. Anything less than this sets us up to misunderstand and disobey. Sixth, emotions aid us in decision making and in pursuing goals.

Before we can have an informed conversation about emotion, we need to ask, What are emotions? How do they work? That's the subject of our next chapter.

Questions for Discussion

1. Would you say that you have been suspicious of emotion? Do you know others who are suspicious? Tell why or why not.
2. Is it difficult for you to discuss emotions? Explain your answer.
3. Have you heard the common statement, "Love is not an emotion, it's an action"? If so, tell what you think the speaker was trying to get at. What do you think of the statement?
4. The author says that "if we have learned anything from the close relationships we have in our lives, we have learned that our friends and family don't want our duty; they want our affection." Has this been your experience? Give an example from your life.
5. The author says that "to learn the most from the Bible, we need to engage it both cognitively and emotionally. Anything less than this sets us up to misunderstand and disobey." Do you agree or disagree? Tell why.

Suggestions for Further Reading

Baker, Robert O. "Pentecostal Bible Reading: Toward a Model of Reading for the Formation of Christian Affections." *Journal of Pentecostal Theology* 7 (1995): 34–48.

Carson, D. A. "Motivations to Appeal to in Our Hearers When We Preach for Conversion." *Themelios* 35, no. 2 (2010): 258–64. The journal *Themelios* is available for free on the Gospel Coalition website (http://thegospelcoalition.org/).

Kuhn, Karl Allen. *The Heart of Biblical Narrative: Rediscovering Biblical Appeal to the Emotions.* Minneapolis: Fortress, 2009.

2 ◆ How Emotions Work

THE QUESTION CAME at around 8:30 on a Thursday morning. "What are you angry about?" I was surprised by the question and speechless for a minute.

Most Thursdays I meet with two to three men over coffee. We talk about life and read a little bit of the New Testament in Greek together. The meeting had just ended when one of the guys—an associate pastor at the church I attend (I'll call him Matt)—asked me this question. He asked the question gently, but it still hit me.

I thought back over our last hour and a half together and suddenly realized that he was right. I had been angry. I had not realized it until he asked me, but it was there still.

How did he see it? I realized I had seemed tense, less joyful, and less patient. These were all external signs of something internal: I was angry. After pondering for a minute or so, the cause came to me. I told Matt that some particularly stressful things were happening lately—things that I thought should not be happening. As a result, I was worried, perplexed, overly busy, and frustrated.

My little "episode" included several telling anger indicators. Those signs suggest how our emotions work.

My emotional indicator: I was not thinking "I am angry." But I was feeling it.

How our emotions work: We typically experience an emotion as a "feeling" we have, as opposed to a thought we have.

My emotional indicator: I was tense and short-tempered.

How our emotions work: Our feelings typically go along with some sort of body experience like "butterflies" in the stomach, a lump in the throat, facial expression, or sweaty palms.

> *My emotional indicator*: I acted like a different person that morning, and Matt could see my different actions.
> *How our emotions work*: Many times, especially if we do not consciously work hard to control it, the emotion will be seen by those around us.

> *My emotional indicator*: I was ignorant of my feelings, until Matt pointed out my anger.
> *How our emotions work:* Sometimes we can be wholly or partially ignorant of our emotional experience.

> *My emotional indicator*: The trigger for my emotional response was things happening that I thought should not be happening.
> *How our emotions work*: Beneath our emotions are causes in our life, whether events, people, or thoughts.

> *My emotional indicator*: Things were happening that I thought should not be happening.
> *How our emotions work*: Emotions are related to beliefs, convictions, or perspectives we have.

THE NATURE OF OUR EMOTIONS

Is an emotion something we feel only in the body—or is it something that also happens in the mind? How does an emotion relate to a thought? As we asked in chapter 1, do emotions come on us willy-nilly like a virus comes on us? Do we just pick them up from the environment?

If we look at it narrowly, an emotion is a feeling experience; it is an affective experience. An emotion is not the same thing as a thought, although emotions and thoughts can be closely related (more on this shortly). Thoughts can be wholly objective and nonemotional, such as the thought that the dark clouds overhead mean rain is likely. Emotions are not experienced in this way but as things highly subjective, very personal, and so very important. From our own experience of emotions, they are often linked to a bodily experience, such as an adrenaline rush, a rapid heartbeat, flushing (turning red). Other neurological elements are likely yet unfelt, such as increased blood flow to, or increased electrochemical activity in certain areas of the brain. Very familiar to us are behavioral or external somatic elements, such as rude hand gestures, tears, hugs, high fives, closing your eyes (I do this on roller coasters).

I accept what is now called a cognitive theory of the emotions.[1] Emotions are closely related to our thinking and especially to how we interpret events in our life, whether an event is good or bad, a blessing or a threat. But in order to interpret something, we need beliefs, convictions, or perspectives.

Here's an example of how this works. Suppose someone carelessly or aggressively cuts us off in heavy traffic and we become angry. Some process like this has happened:

- You have the conviction (belief) that your safety is important.
- You believe you have the right, within reasonable limits, to defend your safety.
- You conclude that the one who carelessly cut you off has threatened this safety for no good reason.

- You then conclude that this is wrong. (Here we begin to see that emotions are closely related to a decision about something good, right, or valuable.)
- You may believe you have the right to express your offense—maybe a verbal criticism (even without a passenger sitting next to you or a long blast of the horn)—or perhaps even exact revenge (if we act on this view, it's called "road rage").
- The feeling of anger (increased heart rate, tension in the face and neck) is a physical corollary to our interpretation that we have been wrongly treated.
- You think, "I'm ticked off." That is, you recognize what has happened in your mind and body. You are angry.

OUR EMOTIONAL RESPONSES: UNCONSCIOUS AND QUICK

This process is logical and cognitive. But even though it is logical and cognitive, it can be a largely unconscious process and a very quick process. Let's consider each of these elements.

Emotions as Unconscious. When I say unconscious, I mean that the emotion process does not require the focus, the attention, and the conscious awareness that we need if we are doing long division with pencil and paper.

Can a logical and thinking process be unconscious? Actually, it happens all the time! Take driving, for example. Driving is a complex process. It involves making all sorts of judgments about your car's speed and balance, about the speeds of other vehicles, about weather conditions, and even about your car's condition (whether it's making a funny noise). But most of this happens below conscious awareness (unless we are driving in a storm). We can go for miles without concentrating on our speed, on the speed of others, or on road conditions.

Similarly, conversation is a complex process. It involves sophisticated interpretations of inflection, word choice, body language, pauses, and the like. But rarely does this interpretation involve conscious processing. We can have an emotion well up in us without our focusing our attention on what is happening.

WITH A JERK, YOU STOP. Your heart is pounding. What just happened?

Emotions as Quick. But even though the emotion process is a logical and cognitive process, it can be a very quick process. Imagine you're on vacation in New York City and are walking downtown. You are talking to a spouse or friend and are quite occupied trying to find your way with a map. Maybe you are looking forward to seeing the Guggenheim Museum. Just before you cross a street, out of the corner of your eye you see something big and noisy. With a jerk, you stop right away. The big and noisy thing is a truck, and you almost got run over because you were about to cross the street without a walk signal. Your heart is pounding and you are shaking. What just happened? In a matter of a couple of seconds:

- You have the conviction that your safety is important.
- You believe you have the right, within reasonable limits, to defend your safety.
- The "big noisy thing" seems threatening.

- You stop suddenly as a way to protect yourself and your spouse/friend.
- Your feelings (increased heart rate, shaking) are a physical corollary to your interpretation that you have been threatened.
- You think, *Wow! That was scary!* That is, you recognize in your mind and body what has happened. You were afraid.

This process is logical and cognitive. But it certainly does not involve us pausing for a few minutes to evaluate the merits of stopping before we get run over. It's a quick process.

WHY OUR EMOTIONS MATTER

What difference does this make? Our emotions are a gauge of what matters most to us. As such, we should not think of them as coming upon us while we are passive, like a virus in a sneak attack. Emotions don't just happen against our will. Rather emotions are those things that arise when there is interaction between our convictions (beliefs) and events in our environment that either threaten us or affirm us. Here are three practical corollaries: Emotions can be evaluated, emotions can be altered or cultivated, and different people have different emotional responses.

Emotions can be evaluated. You might have heard it said, "Emotions are neither good nor bad, they just are." That statement is only true if emotions come on us willy-nilly like a virus. If they are deeply tied to our convictions, then emotions might be right or wrong. For example, when King Herod heard that wise men from the east were asking about one born King of the Jews, "he was troubled, and all Jerusalem with him" (Matthew 2:3). This negative emotion (being troubled) comes about because Herod views this as a threat. After the wise men see the Christ child and depart, an angel warns Joseph, "Rise, take the child and his mother, and flee to Egypt, and remain there until I tell you, for Herod is about to search for the child, to destroy him" (v. 13). Later, when Herod "saw that he had been tricked by the wise men, [he] became furious, and he sent and killed all the male children in Bethlehem and in all that region who were two years old or under" (v. 16). On the one hand, Herod's emotion is totally understandable, even logical. If he is very suspicious and frightened of anyone who might challenge his authority, we can see why he'd be troubled. On the other hand, this is clearly a bad emotion; it is based on pride and arrogance, on a false belief about Jesus.

Similarly, Paul says that love "does not rejoice at wrong-doing" (1 Corinthians 13:6a). Here we have an emotion (joy) that in other places would be good (v. 6b); in this place, however, it is bad. It should not happen. Such "love" is unloving.

Emotions can be altered or cultivated. If we are completely passive in emotions, then there is no hope to change problem emotions; there is no hope to cultivate godly emotions. But if emotions are linked to convictions, then we would expect that as convictions change, so do emotions. Suppose there are two brothers named Loren and Doren. Both brothers profess to be atheists; for many years they mock Jesus, the gospel, and Christians. Then Loren receives Christ. We would expect Loren's emotions to change. Previously when he heard of someone believing the gospel he would mock (as his unbelieving brother Doren still does). Now Loren rejoices to know that there is another worshiper of God. Whereas before if Loren heard of a pastor who fell into moral problems, he would mock (as his unbelieving brother Doren still does), now when he hears of such a thing he mourns. These new emotions are the results of Loren's new convictions.

This illustration does not imply that emotions will always change quickly or that bad ones can always be altered overnight. The process might be very slow.[2] We'll talk more about the slow process of change in upcoming chapters as we explore particular emotions.

Different people have different emotional responses. That's obvious! We've all seen it, but why does it happen? The principle is this: emotional reactions are influenced by a person's individual beliefs or history. Let's go back to the example of being cut off in heavy traffic. Suppose that, years earlier, someone had pulled in front of you suddenly. The outcome was a horrible and painful accident. Now for you the convictions "My safety is important" and "Cutting someone off in traffic is threatening" have taken on new meaning. As a result, when this next driver cuts you off, you probably would find his actions more threatening than I would find them. So the strength or significance of the same conviction can vary from person to person.

Robert Roberts provides a telling example from Ezra 3:10–13. The chapter tells of the Israelites who returned from exile and rebuilt the temple in Jerusalem. Roberts reports that after the temple's foundation was complete, when the people gathered, two differing emotional responses took place:

> One group shouted for joy, the other wept with grief, and both were responding to one situation: the new temple of God emerging in outline as its foundation took shape. Both groups believed the words of praise with which they sang to God: "For he is good, for his steadfast love endures forever toward Israel." How, then, can their emotions be so different, the one group feeling joy, the other grief? The answer is that they saw different things in this situation, or to put the matter another way, they

didn't quite see the same situation, or they didn't see the same meaning in the situation, or they were not seeing the situation from the same angle. By their pleasure, the joyful group saw the coming fulfillment of their fondest hopes, the wonderful goodness of the prospect: to worship God in his holiest place. The grieving group did not deny that prospect, but they saw something different in the emerging figure of the new temple. With vivid pain they saw what they had lost.[3]

Because emotions have cognitive content, the responses may not be the same from person to person. The individual changes over time and his understanding may become more sophisticated in this area.

DETECTING EMOTIONS

That Thursday morning Matt could detect that something was different; rather than being cheerful, I was tense and short-tempered. With his help, I was able to discover this too. This is a normal process. This raises the twin questions: How do I detect emotions in others and How do I detect the emotions in myself?

Detecting emotion in others: Emotion and facial expression go together. That is, we expect to be able to see where people are emotionally from their facial expression—and also by certain words, tone of voice, and body language. Because we associate facial expression and emotion so closely, acting (whether on stage, in motion pictures, or on television) can move us. If we assumed that facial expression and emotion were normally unrelated, we would have very little basis for emotional engagement with a good movie. This is supported by common sense, by personal experience, and by extensive research.[4] We will return to this shortly in the next chapter.

When Paul commands, "Rejoice with those who rejoice, weep with those who weep" (Romans 12:15), clearly he assumes that we can normally detect someone else's emotions through facial expression and body language. As with so many other life skills, this skill might need to be cultivated through practice, and since people are so different, each new acquaintance might challenge our expertise.

Of course, there are other ways of detecting emotion. I'm sure you've received an email that you rightly interpreted as an angry message and no caps were required. A certain choice of words, a terseness, might reflect anger. In contrast, a different choice of words, exclamation points, or an emoticon, might display joy.

Only when a social situation demands it do we break apart an emotion and its expression. Suppose I'm at a funeral during a crucial moment of a solemn eulogy. My mind starts to wander, and I think of a new joke I heard. I can laugh on the inside, but it would not be appropriate for me to burst out laughing (to give the normal emotional show of my glad feeling).

Detecting emotion in ourselves: As my experience with Matt shows, the ability to detect our own emotions can be a challenge. Some of us might have no problem with learning a new smart phone or learning to operate a new Blu-ray player. It might strike us as odd to think we need to learn our emotions. But we do!

Sometimes we do not understand what is going on in ourselves. But, if we are "fearfully and wonderfully made" (Psalm 139:14), then we should not be surprised. Being made in the image of God (Genesis 1:26; James 3:9), we are complex creatures. Life, likewise, is rarely one-dimensional. We might experience a combination of emotions. A good example comes from the life of Jesus. Mark 3:1–6 says,

Again he entered the synagogue, and a man was there

with a withered hand. And they watched Jesus, to see whether he would heal him on the Sabbath, so that they might accuse him.

And he said to the man with the withered hand, "Come here." And he said to them, "Is it lawful on the Sabbath to do good or to do harm, to save life or to kill?" But they were silent. And he looked around at them with anger, grieved at their hardness of heart, and said to the man, "Stretch out your hand." He stretched it out, and his hand was restored. The Pharisees went out and immediately held counsel with the Herodians against him, how to destroy him.

We'll talk more about this passage in the chapter on anger (chapter 5). For now we just notice that Jesus was experiencing two emotions at once: grief and anger. It is not uncommon for us to experience two or more emotions together such as love and joy, or discouragement and anger.

ARE EMOTIONS WORTH IT? A BRIEF LOOK AT JESUS

Perhaps at this point, one might still wonder, "Yeah, but aren't emotions second-rate? Why waste all this time talking about emotions when what God really wants from us is belief [trust] and action?" Let's look into this.

Jesus in the Gospels. The writers of the Gospels indicate they did not tell everything that could be said about Jesus (John 20:30; Luke 1:1–4). There was more to say than could possibly be fit into books (John 21:25)! But the Spirit led them to select certain deeds, acts, and teaching. Each thing selected is important and needed so that we might believe this Jesus, know Him, and live like Him.

In several of His deeds, His emotions are displayed—not just grief and joy, but at times compassion, sadness, and even sorrow.

Becoming like Jesus. What it means to be truly human is to be like Jesus. God's goal is to conform us to His Son (Romans 8:29). Paul commanded, "Be imitators of me, as I am of Christ" (1 Corinthians 11:1). The attitude of Jesus should be our attitude (Philippians 2:5). As we will see later, in His humanity Jesus is comfortable with His emotions.

Jesus—sinless and virtuous. Since with Jesus we are dealing with a sinless man (2 Corinthians 5:20–21; Hebrews 4:15), we can work with the assumption that any emotion we detect with Jesus is a sinless manifestation of the emotion. If He was angry, as we saw in Mark 3, then some anger is sinless anger. If He was sorrowful (Matthew 26:37), there are times when we can experience a sinless sorrow.

IMITATING JESUS means imitating both His action and His emotion.

But we need to go beyond this. "Sinless" is a negative word. While it is correct—and very important—to call Jesus sinless, it really only puts us on a neutral or level place. Rocks and trees have no sin, but they can hardly show us how to live! On the other hand, positively, we can say that all Jesus' thoughts, feelings, and actions are virtuous. The Father said of His Son, "You are my beloved Son; with you I am well pleased" (Luke 3:22). Jesus always did his Father's will (John 5:19, 6:38).

Thus, Jesus is our example not only of bad things to be avoided (sins) but also of good things to be imitated (virtue). To say it again, imitating Jesus means imitating both His action and His emotion.

THE SUM OF OUR FEELINGS

In this chapter I set out basics of the discussion, including some presuppositions from which we must work. Through this brief sketch we've seen the following:

* Emotions may be described as feelings we experience in contrast to thoughts we have.
* But emotions work in conjunction with our beliefs and convictions. To put it simply, our experience is often something like this: conviction + event = emotion.
* Therefore, emotions can be evaluated, altered, and cultivated.
* Emotions typically go along with some sort of body experience, such as increased heart rate, facial expression, or a lump in the throat.
* Most of the time people can detect our emotion by way of our facial expression or body language.
* Emotions are complex. We might experience more than one emotion at a time. Sometimes we can be wholly or partially ignorant of our emotional experience.

Toward a Healthy Emotional Life

As we consider the reasons for and obstacles to a healthy emotional life, this theoretical needs to be practical. So every chapter will conclude with an application section followed by questions for discussion. "Toward a Healthy Emotional Life" begins with four ways to better understand and develop your emotional life.

1. *Pray.* For some of us, recognizing, changing, and cultivating emotions is a brand-new endeavor. Pray for God to reveal the workings of your heart (Psalm 139:23). God knows us better than we do. Pray to have the emotions of Jesus. Pray over these biblical commands: hate evil (Psalm 97:10; Romans 12:9), love kindness (Micah 6:8), be fervent in spirit (Romans 12:11), put away wrath (Colossians 3:8).

2. *Reread Scripture.* Perhaps for a long time you have read the Word thinking only about its commands. Start rereading it, looking for anything that might relate to the emotional life. You might start with the examples from chapter 1: Sarah's fear (Genesis 18:15), Hannah's joy (1 Samuel 2:1), Peter's grief (John 21:17), Paul's despair (2 Corinthians 1:8), and Jesus' anger (Mark 3:5). Meditate on why these servants of God had these emotions.

3. *Ponder your emotions.* If emotions are related to convictions, then pondering our emotional experience can tell us something about what lies behind our emotions. Here are some questions to help you start the process: Have I been discouraged lately? If so, why is that? Have I been unusually tense lately? If so, why is that? Do I feel flat, almost emotionless? If so, why? What convictions and events lie behind these emotions?

4. *Enlist a like-minded friend.* Just as Matt helped me to see that I was angry, so a like-minded friend can help you.

Questions for Discussion

1. Before starting to read this book, what was your perspective on how emotions work? Has your perspective been affirmed, challenged, or changed? Explain your answer.
2. Explain in your own words the cognitive theory of emotion.
3. Reflect on the statement "Emotions can be evaluated."
4. Reread Ezra 3:10–13. In those verses the history of different people resulted in their experiencing different emotions. How would you say that your own history influences the emotions at work in your life today?
5. In your experience, are facial expressions a reliable way to discern someone else's emotion? Tell why or why not.
6. Unpack in your own words what is important about Jesus being both completely sinless and always virtuous.

Suggestions for Further Reading

Allender, Dan B. and Tremper Longman III. *The Cry of the Soul: How Our Emotions Reveal Our Deepest Questions about God.* Colorado Springs: NavPress, 1994.

Borgman, Brian S. *Feelings and Faith: Cultivating Godly Emotions in the Christian Life.* Wheaton: Crossway, 2009.

Roberts, Robert C. *Spiritual Emotions: A Psychology of Christian Virtues.* Grand Rapids: Eerdmans, 2007.

3 ◆ The Fruit of the Spirit Is *Joy*

MY LAST FEW MONTHS before becoming a Christian were tough. I knew my life wasn't right. Guilt, disappointment, and frustration soaked through everything. I did well in studies at the architecture school at the University of Florida, but the prospect of working in the field was not appealing at all. Nothing in life was appealing.

The day before spring term in 1980 I got the telephone number of Alan Godwin, a man who worked for Campus Crusade for Christ (now known as Cru). Since this was long before the days of texting, I called him on the telephone one Sunday evening, introduced myself, and said, "I hear that you explain to people how to become Christians. I don't understand how to do that, and I need somebody to explain it to me."

Alan was a bit surprised but set up a meeting for Wednesday at 10 a.m. We sat on a bench in the quadrangle in front of the main library. There, as crowds of University of Florida students were walking to and from classes, he explained the gospel and I received Christ.

What happened next was joy—an emotional reaction. I had suffered with a sense of guilt and frustration for months; it was like a heavy weight upon my back. My joy rose from a feeling of relief. I felt light as a feather.

I like the definition of joy found at the website dictionary .com: "Joy: the emotion of great delight or happiness caused by something good or beneficial."[1] For me, the beneficial element of my spiritual salvation was a newfound sense of peace and security (conviction). Whereas before I felt no purpose for life and was feeling guilty for sins, all of a sudden, having believed the gospel of forgiveness and God having a wonderful plan for my life, I had a different emotion. This is what I would call a spiritual joy.

OUR HUMAN JOYS

For men and women alike, joy comes in different types. One type is our *human joys*. By "human" rejoicing, I mean joy that any human can experience, Christian and non-Christian.

There are many examples. There's the joy of entertaining family and guests. Twice a year my wife and I invite about twenty students to our home for a cookout. The students are happy to get off campus and away from the city, to have some home-cooked food, to play Frisbee or badminton, and to just relax. And my wife and I take pleasure (joy) in serving, sharing their enthusiasm and zest for life, and hearing all about their families and their dreams.

There is wedding joy. One of our daughters recently wed. Anyone who has worked to plan a wedding knows the months of preparation with labor, details, and worries. When our daughter's ceremony and reception were over, we looked back with joy at the grace of God that it all went well, our friends and family had a good time—and that we didn't have to go into debt to make it happen!

Of course, there is jubilation when a child is born: "When a woman is giving birth, she has sorrow because her hour has come, but when she has delivered the baby, she no longer remembers the anguish, for joy that a human being has been born into the world" (John 16:21).

There is the joy of finding something of great value. Jesus described a shepherd who rejoiced over finding one lost sheep, even though ninety-nine were safely home: "If he finds [the missing sheep], truly, I say to you, he rejoices over it more than over the ninety-nine that never went astray" (Matthew 18:13).

Joy also appears wherever people thrive. Under the leadership of Solomon, "Judah and Israel were as many as the sand by the sea. They ate and drank and were happy." Their joy came from their peace, security, and prosperity (1 Kings 4:20). Psalm 104 is an excellent example of the goodness of human thriving— indeed, the thriving of all creation: humans, animals, and plants. From the Psalm we learn that:

- God created the earth and all things in it (vv. 5, 19), and He continues to sustain the earth and all things in it by the loving exercise of His sovereign power (vv. 10–11, 14, 28–29).
- The earth and all things in it belong to God by virtue of His creative work (v. 24), and all things find their reason for being fundamentally in relation to Him (vv. 27–30).
- Even after the entrance of sin into the created order (death, v. 29), this perfection still shines through so as to be perceivable by man (v. 24). Thus, creation continually bears witness to the perfections of God and promotes in man praise toward God (vv. 33–34).[2]

The teaching here is very similar to that in a few other Psalms, including 136:25: "[God] gives food to all flesh, for his steadfast love endures forever" and 132:15: "I will abundantly bless her provisions; I will satisfy her poor with bread." (See also 85:12 and 145:15–16.)

Our definition of joy is "the emotion of great delight or happiness caused by something good or beneficial." It is certainly *better* for a person to thank God for thriving, health, family, good food, and honest work. Nevertheless, it is *good* for people, even non-Christian people, to find joy in these things. The apostle Paul is in agreement when, evangelizing the Lycaonians, he says, God "did not leave himself without witness, for he did good by giving you rains from heaven and fruitful seasons, satisfying your hearts with food and gladness" (Acts 14:17). Better to thank God, but good to find joy.

OUR SPIRITUAL JOYS

Spiritual joys work the same way that normal human joys do, they just have a different object. I call these joys "spiritual" because they are spiritually discerned; that is, we would have no idea how valuable they are for us unless God had made it clear by His Holy Spirit. Thus joy is the Spirit's fruit (Galatians 5:22–23).

In the case of a parent and child, we could lay it out like this:

* As parents, we have the conviction (belief) that the welfare of our children is important.
* As parents who are Christians, we believe that the greatest kind of welfare is having eternal life.
* As Christian parents, we believe that eternal life is found only in Christ (1 John 5:11–12).
* Our children receive Christ.
* We rejoice because they have received something precious (or as the marketers for MasterCard would say, "priceless").

Such rejoicing has its basis in spiritual benefits. Significantly, one of Scripture's major emphases is on spiritual causes of rejoicing. Consider the joy that is found upon receiving *forgiveness* (Psalm 32:1–2), the singing at *a public dedication* (Nehemiah

12:43, dedicating Jerusalem's new wall), taking pleasure in *the sovereign work of God* (Luke 10:21), seeing *sinners repent* (Luke 15:7), or seeing *Christians walking in truth* (2 John 4). Spiritual joy, as with most other emotions, can be either the disposition of a continuing situation (long term; e.g., 2 Corinthians 6:10), or could be based on a certain immediate event (short term; e.g., 2 Corinthians 7:6–7).

A friend of ours tells the story of her marriage. Her husband was not a Christian. For many years he was very hard to live with. He was unhappy, harsh, and demeaning. Then he was gloriously converted. Over the years he has developed patience, the ability to serve, listening skills, and a godly love for his wife. She thanks God for this transformation and rejoices in His grace over this long-term disposition.

Joy can display itself as either long term or short term. With long-term joy, we have a person who says to herself, *Life is good.* Thus her disposition is toward joy; joy is the typical or characteristic experience of her days. With short-term joy, we have a person who says, *This event is good.* That is, because she interprets a particular thing as beneficial, helpful, or leading to peace and security, her reaction is joyful. But once the effects of the event are over, joy subsides or disappears.

We draw this type of distinction all the time. We might talk about being healthy as the general tendency of our life (long term), even if we sometimes get a bad cold (short term). We might talk about having an easygoing personality (long term), even if we do—rarely—get angry (short term). We'll talk more about long- and short-term joy later.

WHAT IS THE ROLE OF CIRCUMSTANCES?
A DIFFERENT VIEW

The perspective on joy that I am describing runs contrary to a very common view. Some say that feeling glad about food, health, or the birth of a child, is not Christian joy. They say that Christian joy has nothing to do with circumstances, that it is a continuous 24/7 experience, and that it is an internal conviction that might not be seen on the outside. Their reasoning could go something like this:

"Only God can offer real peace. Peace and joy will come from knowing the God who made us. He has begotten us. He is our Father; He watches over us and protects us. He manages the universe well. We are friends of God. So then we ought not to sit around sorrowful and groaning, blind to God our great helper or worse yet blaming and complaining against Him. On the other hand, we ought to know God better, to be of one mind with Him, have fellowship with Him, to be His follower and servant.

"We should imitate God. Since God is faithful, so we should be faithful. Since He is generous, so we should be generous. He is happy, so we should be happy. If we really know God, here are the results: We will be free, we will keep our wills in harmony with what God brings into our lives. We will regard God's will as better than our own will. We will not be fearful or grieving, we will not be sorrowful, we will not be anxious; we will have no rage and no envy. Rather, because of knowing God, we will be at peace, we will live a life of joy, we will be content, we will give thanks to God in all things."

The previous two paragraphs might sound like Christianity, but they are not. They are paganism. They echo the teaching of the first-century stoic philosopher Epictetus. If the above sounds like Christianity, it is only because so much teaching about

Christianity and emotion relies on logic and not on the teaching of Scripture.

Scripture does not support the perspective that says Christian joy has nothing to do with circumstances, that it is a continuous, 24/7 experience, and that it is an internal conviction that might not be seen on the outside. To explain, we'll look at two key verses on joy: Romans 12:15 and Philippians 4:4.

"Rejoice with those who rejoice, weep with those who weep" (Romans 12:15). Notice that the passage does not read: "Rejoice with those who rejoice and tell those who weep why they shouldn't." This key verse presupposes a couple of things. It presupposes that we are able, at least to a degree, to recognize rejoicing or weeping in people. In other words, this passage speaks against the common Christian-stoic view that rejoicing can be wholly invisible, wholly submerged. How can I rejoice with someone if I don't see the joy? Somehow you need to be able to see that the person is rejoicing. And it is unlikely that you'll rely only on the person's words (that is, you will also use facial expression and body language). If your friend has a sad face and sluggish movement and looks disheveled, and she says, "I am really rejoicing today," you would recognize that something has gone wrong.

Romans 12:15 further presupposes that we can distinguish between true rejoicing and weeping. Obviously, weeping and rejoicing are different! And, obviously again, we do not distinguish them only by the words people say. We do so by discerning the meaning of facial expression and body language. If we recognize that our friend is rejoicing, we have no reason to believe that he is "weeping on the inside" (unless we know him to be deceptive). That is, unless there is good reason to think otherwise, we take the external signs to give faithful indication of what is going on inside. So likewise, if we recognize that our friend is weeping, we have no reason to believe he is "rejoicing on the inside" (again, unless we know him to be deceptive). *Thus Romans 12:15 presupposes that rejoicing is normally seen on the outside.*

ROMANS 12:15 *requires* empathy, which is a sign of maturity, of love, and a ministry skill.

Romans 12:15 not only *presupposes* that we can see rejoicing and distinguish it from mourning, it *requires* empathy, which has been defined as "the vicarious experiencing of the feelings, thoughts, or attitudes of another."[3] Empathy is a sign of maturity, of love, and a ministry skill. Paul commands empathy. Thus, in a sense, emotion can be commanded. At a funeral it would be easy to quote Romans 8:28 to a grieving spouse. If you do so, I hope those around you have the courage to tell you that you are not being helpful. At a funeral, "weep with those who weep" is much more appropriate.

Now before we go on, we need to acknowledge that there are times when we can be exempt from this command in Romans 12:15. But these times would be the exceptions, not the rule. So 1 Corinthians 13:6 says that love "does not rejoice at wrongdoing." So we will not rejoice together with a Christian brother because he just robbed a bank and now has $6,000 to pay off his overdue bills. We will not rejoice together with a Christian teen because so far his parents haven't found out he regularly accesses pornography on his iPhone. But again, those are exceptions.[4]

Further, we do not empathize absentmindedly. Mature empathy is self-reflective. That is, I will be aware that I am empathizing. I will know that I feel joy or distress, not because of my own life, but because of someone else's.[5]

"Rejoice in the Lord always; again I will say, rejoice" (Philippians 4:4): This well-known verse has been the rescue for many who were suffering discouragement. How often does a Christian have good cause for rejoicing? All the time! There's joy in past salvation; there's joy in forgiveness of sins; there's joy in the love of God in Christ—a love beyond comprehension (Ephesians 3:19). There's joy in God's current work in us, transforming our hardships into proven character (Romans 5:4). There's joy when we ponder the eternal glory God has promised to us (Romans 8:30).

THANKFULLY, WE ARE not forced to choose between continuous external cheerfulness and hidden internal joy.

But does Paul mean by "rejoice in the Lord always" that rejoicing must happen every minute of every day? If we draw that conclusion, we will be stuck in a hard place between two things that won't work. Either, on the one side, we will think that joy has no emotional content and so can be happening "on the inside" while on the outside I am grieving the abuse of children, or the loss of a nonbelieving spouse, or the great pain of cancer. Or, on the other side, we will think that joy has emotional content, is seen "on the outside," and therefore, since Paul commands "rejoice always," a Christian can never show anger, or sorrow, or fear. But clearly both of these options will not fit with Romans 12:15: *rejoicing is seen* and *there are times when weeping is appropriate.*

So where do we go from here? Thankfully, we are not forced to choose between continuous external cheerfulness and hidden internal joy. There is a third option, which becomes clear if we look at Paul's word for *always*. Sometimes this word refers to something that happens continuously (24/7). For example, Jesus says He always does His Father's will (John 8:29), and that the Father always hears Him (John 11:42). Hebrews says that Jesus always lives to make intercession for us (7:25). What blessed truths these are! Without the continuous life of Jesus, we would all be sunk.

On the other hand, this same word Paul uses for "always" sometimes refers to things that happen often or typically. For example, during His trial Jesus was questioned about His teaching and about His disciples. He responded, "I have spoken openly to the world. I have always taught in synagogues and in the temple, where all Jews come together" (John 18:20). "Always" here must mean typically or characteristically, since we know from Matthew 5:1 that Jesus gave a lengthy sermon on the side of a mountain. Even in Philippians, the great epistle of joy, Paul mentions that while writing he wept over enemies of the cross (3:18). Finally, in 2 Corinthians 5:6 Paul said, "So we are always of good courage." Earlier in this same letter, however, he mentioned his great despair (1:8). So we should understand that courage was a long-term characteristic of his life, not his continuous experience.

THE SUM OF OUR FEELINGS

Joy should be characteristic of our life; it should be our typical experience. This joy will have emotional content; it will be felt. Primarily, this joy will be based on the work that God has already accomplished for us in Christ. Since this Jesus loves us intensely and since He "is the same yesterday and today and forever" (Hebrews 13:8), there is always a reason to rejoice. But our rejoicing will also be based on occasional human and spiritual goods, such as the restoration of a marriage, a sunset, or the pleasure of a good meal with friends. Let's not forget, too, that this joy will be seen. Our non-Christian neighbors will not find a submerged joy appealing.

If we have times of pain, weeping, or anxiety, that does not mean we have failed to obey the command of Philippians 4:4. It might mean instead that we have obeyed the command of Romans 12:15.

Toward a Healthy Emotional Life

1. *Start with the Lord.* To experience personal joy, we cannot start with ourselves; we must start with the Lord. Ponder and pray over the love of God in Christ. Good passages for this include Matthew 27:27–54, Romans 8:18–39, Ephesians 3:15–19, and Philippians 2:5–11. One of my favorites is Revelation 21:3–4: "And I heard a loud voice from the throne saying, 'Behold, the dwelling place of God is with man. He will dwell with them, and they will be his people, and God himself will be with them as their God. He will wipe away every tear from their eyes, and death shall be no more, neither shall there be mourning, nor crying, nor pain anymore.'"

2. *Take joy in God's present provision.* As we said, regular human joys are good. We should allow ourselves to enjoy a sunset, time with a close friend, a job well done, a good meal. 1 Timothy 6:17 says that God "richly provides us with everything to enjoy." So enjoying God's daily provision is godly.

3. *Slay the joy killers.* Some emotions can be killers of joy At times anger and anxiety are totally appropriate. But long-term anger or anxiety can yield a joyless life. Likewise, there are godly forms of jealousy (Exodus 34:14; 2 Corinthians 11:2); but most of the time our jealousy is massively selfish. Long-term jealousy can really squelch joy. So in addition to cultivating joy positively, we can cultivate it negatively by slaying our joy killers. For help, check "Toward a Healthy Emotional Life" at the end of chapters 4, 5, and 6.

4. *Feel joy for the successes of others.* Life isn't competition; we can rejoice with others when they enjoy good things. Remember

Paul's words to those in Lystra. He wrote, God "did not leave himself without witness, for he did good by giving you rains from heaven and fruitful seasons, satisfying your hearts with food and gladness" (Acts 14:17). Even if you have an in-law who doesn't like you, you can rejoice with him when he boasts about how great his vacation was. Even if your boss is a tyrant, you can rejoice with her when her children do well in school or sports.

Questions for Discussion

1. The author says that, "normal human rejoicing is good." Do you agree or disagree? Tell why.
2. Have you heard of the opinion that says, "Christian joy has nothing to do with circumstances, that it is a continuous 24/7 experience, and that it is an internal conviction that might not be seen on the outside"? What do you see as the advantages of such a perspective? What are the disadvantages?
3. Reread the short section taken from Epictetus, the pagan philosopher (under the section "A Different View"). What is your reaction to his perspective? Do you find his perspective surprising? Explain.
4. Explain in your own words what it would look like to rejoice with those who rejoice (Romans 12:15). Have you experienced it?
5. Share with the group your biggest joy killer. Seek their help in dealing with it.

Suggestions for Further Reading

Piper, John. *The Dangerous Duty of Delight*. Portland: Multnomah, 2001.

Smith, William P. "Celebrating Love: Rejoicing with Each Other," chapter 13 in *Loving Well*. Greensboro, NC: New Growth Press, 2012.

4 ♦ If I'm Forgiven, Why Do I Feel *Guilt and Shame?*

I WAS STANDING near the fifty-yard line of Pro Player Stadium, home of the Miami Dolphins. The sweat poured down my face as I stood saluting at full attention. The noise of the crowd was deafening.

It was September 23, 2001, the Dolphins' first home game after the 9/11 terrorist attacks on America. The director of special events (I'll call him Peter) had decided to have a special patriotic pregame ceremony. Members of the United States Army, Air Force, Navy, Marine Corps, and Coast Guard were all on the field. The U.S. Army's 82nd Airborne All-American Chorus had finished their performance. (Those guys can really sing!)

As a chaplain of the Air Force Reserve, I had been asked to pray. Of course I was nervous, and the south Florida heat was taking its toll. My assignment was to come onto a small platform at midfield and pray for about forty-five seconds. I recall that Peter told me—or at least I thought that I remembered he told me—that after I prayed I was supposed to step off to the side of the platform and then the National Anthem would play. Somehow, with a TV camera arm's length away from me, I managed to pray and then stepped off. I heard music and so immediately went to attention and saluted.

What happened next? Well, it was not the National Anthem. Music was playing while large monitors in the stadium showed footage of the planes crashing into the towers. There were brief clips of people who escaped. I began to think to myself, "I look stupid! I should not be saluting; it's not the National Anthem!" But then I thought, "But I'll look even stupider if I put the salute down now!"

So the debate continued inside my head: *Up or down?* My worry: which one would look less stupid? I am thinking that 80,000 people are looking at me saying to themselves, "This guy doesn't even recognize the melody to our National Anthem." My worry was idolatrous: I wanted all to see that I was strong, competent, in control. But I failed.

After what seemed like an eternity (maybe five or six minutes), the Anthem finally began. The sweat dripped off my nose as I anxiously waited for it to be over. That's my signal to march off the field. And march off I did; as fast as possible, feeling utterly ashamed and embarrassed.

What is this feeling called *shame*? Where does it come from? Is it good?

THE DIFFERENCE
BETWEEN GUILT AND SHAME

Guilt and *shame*. These two emotions are closely related and sometimes they overlap in our lives in ways that make them hard to distinguish. Furthermore, the way that Scripture uses the terms is not the way we typically use them. That is okay. Following the wording of Scripture is good, but we don't need to always imitate its wording. We just need to realize how our conversation relates to what Scripture talks about. For definition, let's start.

What is guilt and what does it mean to feel guilty? Guilt involves the belief that we have done something wrong (some sin). It also involves an unpleasant feeling of remorse or regret, a highly subjective heaviness or darkness. We may worry that we might face punishment or other negative results. When we experience this, we say we are "feeling guilty." Typically we believe that we have broken God's law or some other requirement placed on us by friends, family, or authorities.

When we feel guilty, the guilt is toward the person we injured—not a generalized guilt toward every person we encounter. When guilt arises, we typically want forgiveness: that is, we want the injured party to know our guilt, to forgive us (release all right to punish), and to welcome us back to previous standing.

What is shame or feeling ashamed? Shame might involve the belief that we have done something wrong (guilt), but it does not have to. Shame is an emotion similar to embarrassment. Embarrassment typically has to do with how we feel when we are exposed as weak or helpless. The incident may not have been our fault, but it still makes us look weak or incompetent. It's often a public feeling. But embarrassment need not involve guilt for moral wrong (some wrong action in my past). Shame is a more personal assessment. I might feel guilty for a wrong action; I feel ashamed of what I am—a person who does wrong things. The kind of shame we want to talk about is often connected with guilt. It can be public. But it can also be intensely private: a powerfully negative sense of our own worth, strength, competence, lovability, or morality (holiness).

THE SCRIPTURES ON GUILT

Legal Guilt. If we search our Bible for the words *guilt* or *guilty*, we will get a lot of helpful verses. All of these, however, talk about a legal position, not an emotional experience. When Scripture uses the terms *guilt* or *guilty*, it's like a jury passing the verdict "guilty." It has to do with an objective position before the law, the liability to punishment.

For example, here are three Bible passages that describe judgment.

Deuteronomy 24:15 commands that a hired laborer must be paid his wages at the end of the day, "before the sun sets (for he is poor and counts on it), lest he cry against you to the Lord, and you be guilty of sin." Failure to pay means the boss faces God's punishment.

2 Chronicles 24:18 shows the judgment that came upon the people of Judah for leaving worship of Jehovah. "They abandoned the house of the Lord, the God of their fathers, and served the Asherim and the idols. And wrath came upon Judah and Jerusalem for this guilt of theirs." God's wrath, His personal and holy reaction, came upon those who engaged in (were guilty of) idolatry.

Luke 23:1–4 describes the judgment rendered by the first-century governor over Jerusalem. After the crowd accused Jesus of "forbidding us to give tribute to Caesar, and saying that he himself is Christ, a king," Pilate asked Jesus, "'Are you the King of the Jews?' And he answered him, 'You have said so.' Then Pilate said to the chief priests and the crowds, 'I find no guilt in this man.'" To 'find no guilt' does not refer to Pilate seeing Jesus' feelings; rather, Pilate finds no evidence that Jesus did evil. Therefore, before the Law, Jesus was not guilty.

Emotional Guilt. Closer to what we mean by guilt feelings would be other Bible passages that use words other than *guilt* or *guilty* to describe the experience we have.

Psalm 32:1–5 describes the feelings of forgiveness King David experienced: "Blessed is the one whose transgression is forgiven, whose sin is covered. Blessed is the man against whom the Lord counts no iniquity, and in whose spirit there is no deceit. For when I kept silent, my bones wasted away through my groaning all day long. For day and night your hand was heavy upon me; my strength was dried up as by the heat of summer. Selah. I acknowledged my sin to you, and I did not cover my iniquity; I said, 'I will confess my transgressions to the Lord,' and you forgave the iniquity of my sin."

Here King David might be referring to the sin he committed

against Bathsheba and Uriah (2 Samuel 11:1–27). But no matter the historical situation, the way he describes his experience of sin, conviction, and forgiveness is typical of our experience.

GOD GIVES US this emotion of guilt to prompt us to take the appropriate action: repentance.

The phrase "when I kept silent" refers to a time before repentance, when David was keeping his sin to himself; he had yet to confess. At that point, he felt the hand of God on him. We would call this *conviction*. David describes it in a way we can relate to. Guilt feels like a heaviness; David says God's "hand was heavy upon" him. If the sin is especially bad, the grief of it can sap our strength as the "heat of summer" can do.

Acts 2:14–37 recounts the day of Pentecost, when Peter preached to a mixed audience in Jerusalem. The apostle rebuked the crowd for their cruel rejection of Jesus (2:23, 36). But now they listened and responded: "Now when they heard this they were cut to the heart, and said to Peter and the rest of the apostles, 'Brothers, what shall we do?'" That is, coming to realize that they are guilty of rejecting Jesus Messiah, they have a painful emotional reaction ("cut to the heart") and know that something must be done. Peter commands them to repent in order that they might be forgiven.

In *2 Corinthians 7:8–10* the apostle Paul describes to the Corinthian believers the result of their sins—sins for which he had strongly rebuked them in an earlier letter (see 2 Corinthians 1:23–2:9). "For even if I made you grieve with my letter, I do not regret it—though I did regret it, for I see that that letter grieved you, though only for a while. As it is, I rejoice, not because you were grieved, but because you were grieved into repenting. For you felt a godly grief, so that you suffered no loss through us. For godly grief produces a repentance that leads to salvation without regret, whereas worldly grief produces death."

Here Paul describes the guilt feelings of the Corinthians in a way not found in Psalm 32 or Acts 2. Guilt is a kind of grief, a painful negative emotion. God gives us this emotion as a way of prompting us to take the appropriate action: repentance.

THE SCRIPTURES ON SHAME

In contrast to guilt, when Scripture mentions shame it has to do with being found foolish, weak, and vulnerable, or with the threat of being found so. Sin is not necessarily involved.

David calls out to God in *Psalm 25:1–3*: "To you, O Lord, I lift up my soul. O my God, in you I trust; let me not be put to shame; let not my enemies exult over me. Indeed, none who wait for you shall be put to shame; they shall be ashamed who are wantonly treacherous."

As king, David led Israel's armies but often faced difficult battles with powerful and treacherous enemies (e.g., Psalms 5:8, 17:9, 56:1–3, 69:18). Who will be victorious? The thought of being defeated militarily leads him to thoughts of possible shame. That is, in defeat David will be shown as weak (he is less capable than the enemy), as vulnerable to threat, pain, brutality (enemies could torture him), and as foolish in his trusting God (his God was too weak to save). These three are common fears: weak, vulnerable, foolish. Thoughts of weakness oppose our desire to be strong and in control. Thoughts of vulnerability cripple us with fear of being exploited. Thoughts of foolishness attack our deepest sense of what is good and trustworthy. With David's psalm we see only the threat of shame; in Jeremiah's life, we see the threat materialized. Jeremiah preached that Israel needed to repent of its apostasy and idolatry or else it would face annihilation by Babylon (e.g., Jeremiah 19:1–9). In *Jeremiah 20:1–18*, the shame is at the request of a supposed man of God. Pashhur the priest has heard Jeremiah's preaching and orders that the prophet be beaten and locked overnight in the stocks that were in the upper Benjamin Gate of the house of the Lord. This was bloody, lengthy, and public humiliation. As a result of this painful abuse, Jeremiah cries out to the Lord with a bitter lament (20:7–10, 14–18) that reveals how deeply hurt he was—both physically and emotionally.

LIKE THE PROPHET Jeremiah, Paul is persecuted for his message. Yet he declares: "I am not ashamed of the gospel."

At the very end, Jeremiah bemoans his situation. "Why did I come out from the womb to see toil and sorrow, and spend my days in shame?" (v. 18). Unlike King David who fears becoming weak, vulnerable, and foolish, Jeremiah experiences these outcomes. He is weak because he cannot defend himself nor convince people with his words and vulnerable because others can take command of his body and lock him up. He is foolish because, in the view of the people around him, his message, and his God proved worthless and incapable.

In *Romans 1:16:* Paul, like the prophet Jeremiah, is persecuted for his message, even to the point of being beaten and locked up (e.g., Acts 16:18–24). Yet he declares: "I am not ashamed of the gospel, for it is the power of God for salvation to everyone who believes, to the Jew first and also to the Greek" (compare 2 Timothy 1:8). Why doesn't Paul's experience lead to deeply painful feelings of being weak, vulnerable, and foolish?

The answer is that Paul's definition of weak, vulnerable, and foolish has been transformed by Jesus and the gospel:

- *Weak.* Paul realizes he can live in the power of God, just as his Savior does. There is a paradox here. On the one hand, Jesus died in weakness, but He "lives by the power of God" (2 Corinthians 13:4). In addition, Paul says, "For the sake of Christ, then, I am content with weaknesses, insults, hardships, persecutions, and calamities. For when I am weak, then I am strong" (2 Corinthians 12:10).
- *Vulnerable.* Paul views the vulnerability of his body as an opportunity to identify with Christ the servant. Paul regarded his physical persecution as sharing the sufferings of Jesus (Philippians 3:10). This is a common theme for Paul (Romans 8:17; Galatians 6:17; Colossians 1:24; 2 Timothy 2:8–10).
- *Foolish.* Paul knows his preaching can and does change lives, so his actions are wise, not foolish. Most Jews and Greeks viewed the gospel as foolish; for them a crucified Messiah or a crucified Lord was a contradiction (1 Corinthians 1:21–25). Nevertheless, Paul saw many accept this gospel and be radically transformed by it, for the gospel is powerful (Romans 1:16).

HOW GOD USES OUR GUILT AND SHAME

To return to the title of this chapter: If we are forgiven, why do we feel guilt and shame? This is a hard question to answer, since each person's life is unique. There could be a great variety of reasons. But here is some guidance as you think about the answer to why God permits guilt and shame.

Guilt. As a way to help, we can think of our relationship with God like a marriage. It is a secure covenant bond; our place before God is eternally secure. The forgiveness we receive when we trust the gospel is escape from wrath of the coming day of the Lord. We could call this the forgiveness of salvation. On the other hand, a marriage also involves regular confession, repentance, and reconciliation. For the relationship to be daily joyful and helpful, the husband and wife do not just rely on the fact that the relation is permanent. One seeks openness.

It's the same way with God. Our regular confession, repentance, and reconciliation keep us walking with Him, preserves joy in the relationship, and makes us fruitful. We could call this the forgiveness of sanctification. We have eternal forgiveness that assures heaven (salvation). We have daily forgiveness as we confess to the Father, assuring restoration as we continue on the path to be more like Christ (sanctification).

In sanctification, guilt feelings can be very helpful. We are more sinful than we know; holiness is a long path. If we have sinned, it is a blessing when the Holy Spirit convicts us about our sins, as He did with the hearers of Peter's sermon in Acts 2. Feelings of guilt are an invitation; they should lead us to pray, converse with God, and have Him search our hearts. How did we sin? When God makes clear a specific sin or bad attitude, it's our call to come to confess, talk to Him about what motivated us, and remind ourselves of His forgiveness (1 John 1:9).

FEELINGS OF GUILT are an invitation to
pray, converse with God, and have Him
search our hearts.

On the other hand, we might have a generalized feeling of guilt. It might plague us day by day while we cannot pinpoint what in particular we might have done to bring on guilt. We should be very careful with generalized feelings of guilt. We aren't omniscient; we are not wise and insightful enough to know all our sins. It might mean a lengthy period of prayer and godly counsel from those we respect in order for us to finally discern where we are going wrong. But we need to keep in mind that the Enemy would have us feel generally guilty about nothing in particular. Such guilt will rob us of joy and weaken our service for God.

Shame. Causes for shame, and reactions to shameful feelings, are as different as the individual. Each of us, through prayer, counsel, and the guidance of the Word, will need to discern the causes of shame. Here are just three possibilities to prompt your thinking:

First, *shame might be caused by a long battle with sin.* The feelings have moved beyond occasional feelings of guilt for the wrong done, to a deep sense of shame about my own sinfulness. *Why can't I defeat my sin? What's wrong with me?* I have moved from a focus on the bad deed I did to the conclusion that I am a bad person. With this shift I am almost certainly feeling hopeless.

Second, *shame might be caused by abuse* suffered at the hands of someone who ought to love and care for us. Such abuse can leave us feeling deeply damaged and unlovable, convinced that what we have become is hideous or repulsive.[1] The pain of abuse can be physical or it may be verbal. Either way, with repeated abuse we believe the lie that we are unlovable or worthless, convinced that what we have become is hideous or repulsive.

Third, *shame might be caused by long-lasting grief over my disappointment* with my own capabilities or accomplishments. I had exciting goals; I had been seeking a sense of purpose in life; I wanted to make a unique contribution to the world. But I accomplished none of this. I was made in the image of God to represent Him on earth, but I have failed. I am left feeling incompetent or worthless.

If such shame develops, how might we react? We might put a great emotional distance between ourselves and others so that they would not come to know us well enough to see that we are vulnerable, weak, or foolish. That, of course, is counterproductive. We isolate ourselves from those who might be able to help. Others who feel shame might respond with anger. They could use this anger to put themselves in a position of control. The thought of not being in control is too threatening.

Neither of these reactions to shame is ultimately helpful; they just lead us farther into pain and farther away from others. Instead, every instance of shame should lead to greater reliance on and appreciation for the grace of God.[2]

THE SUM OF OUR FEELINGS

Most often, when Scripture uses the term *guilt* or *guilty*, it has to do not with feelings but with something objective, like being found guilty before the judge. In contrast, when people describe themselves as feeling guilty, they are dealing with powerful negative feelings about what they have done. A man or woman regrets a careless act, a malicious thought, an insulting word. When you or I feel guilty we are seeking forgiveness: we want the person we wronged to know our guilt feelings, to give up all right to revenge, and to welcome us back into fellowship.

Closely related to guilt is shame. Both guilty feelings and feelings of shame can have to do with some act we committed. But shame is typically much more personal and much more painful. With shame I have moved beyond regret for an act to a deep sense of dissatisfaction with who I am. The idol I make myself into wanted to be seen as powerful, safe, and wise. But the reverse happened; I am shown to be weak, vulnerable, and foolish. Shame leads us to think such thoughts as, "I am worthless," "I am hideous," or "I am unlovable."

As we will see below, the love of God in Christ is our primary recourse when we are guilty or ashamed. There is hope because He took our guilt and suffered our shame.

Toward a Healthy Emotional Life

Only the gospel of our Lord Jesus Christ can help us with guilt and shame. In contrast, if we insist on being strong (instead of weak), on being invulnerable (instead of vulnerable), and on being capable (instead of foolish), we will never embrace the gospel. It was while we were weak and helpless enemies of God that Jesus died for us (Romans 5:6–10). Here are three action steps that can help you deal with guilt and shame.

1. *Be sure to pray, every day.* Make it your goal to pray daily through Ephesians 3:14–19. These verses remind us that the love of Christ for us is so great as to be beyond comprehension. As God's children we are not loathsome; we are not repulsive because we have been damaged. God does not shun us as foolish. We are His creation. He welcomes us because of the love of Christ.

2. *Ponder the shame that Jesus endured.* Hebrews 12:1–2 reminds us, "Therefore, since we are surrounded by so great a cloud of witnesses, let us also lay aside every weight, and sin which clings so closely, and let us run with endurance the race that is set before us, looking to Jesus, the founder and perfecter of our faith, who for the joy that was set before him endured the cross, despising the shame, and is seated at the right hand of the throne of God." Other passages include Isaiah 50:6–8, 53:3–8; 2 Corinthians 8:9, 13:4; Philippians 2:5–11.

3. *Trust the gospel declared in Scripture.* Far too often I am ashamed because I would like to be more capable, be smarter, more efficient, and more successful. When this happens, I have ceased to worship and trust God. Instead I am worshiping and

trusting myself; I have become my own idol. That is the opposite of the gospel. A works salvation says, "I am capable." The gospel says, "God accepts the weak, the vulnerable, and the incapable."

Questions for Discussion

1. In your own words, tell what you think is the difference between guilt feelings and shame feelings. Are they totally different? Do they overlap?
2. Which one of these two—guilt or shame—would you say that you experience the most? Explain your answer.
3. Have you ever asked yourself the question, "If I am forgiven, why do I feel guilt and shame?" Give an example of a time you did this.
4. Read Jeremiah 20:1–18. Explain, in your own words, what brought Jeremiah to such emotional pain.
5. Weakness, vulnerability, and foolishness: which one of these is typically the cause of your shame feelings? Explain.
6. The author says, "Far too often I am ashamed because I would like to be more capable, be smarter, more efficient, and more successful. When this happens, I have ceased to worship and trust God. Instead I am worshiping and trusting myself; I have become my own idol." Do you agree or disagree? Discuss.

Suggestions for Further Reading

Allender, Dan and Tremper Longman III. *The Cry of the Soul: How Our Emotions Reveal Our Deepest Questions about God.* Colorado Springs: NavPress, 1994.

5 ◆ In My Family, We Never Talked about *Anger*

IT'S HARD TO KNOW how it all started. Maybe one guy wasn't paying attention and got a little too close. Maybe someone was in a hurry. But in the end, Alan was dead. The news headline read: "Wisconsin man gets 25 years for road-rage murder on Edens." The subhead read, "Killer stabbed fellow trucker in fight on expressway's shoulder."[1]

David Seddon and Alan Lauritzen were truckers who encountered each other on the Edens Expressway near Chicago. Somehow the encounter turned vicious. They "sparred over their CB radios and cut each other off in traffic." Finally they decided to make the encounter face-to-face. But after they pulled off to the side of the road, Seddon stabbed Lauritzen to death.

We all know anger when we see it. Our experience—and this news report—tell us in no uncertain terms that anger out of control is scary and dangerous. Likewise, anger is one of the most common emotions. We cannot escape feelings of anger. Why? Your life and mine are characterized by great expectations, by busyness, overwork, aggressiveness by others, disappointment in others and ourselves, greed, and a strong lack of contentment that go along with these expectations. Unfortunately, often our self-worth is based on acquisition and social accomplishment.

Even though our anger is common, we typically find that anger is a difficult subject to talk about. Our anger is at times embarrassing. The anger of others makes us uncomfortable. It's threatening. We may run from it.

In the face of anger, all real communication typically shuts down. That's the way it was in my house growing up. We always knew when someone was angry; the facial expression, body language, and tone of voice gave it away. But rarely was anger talked about. If it was, the only conversation was to blame someone else for your anger.

Why didn't we talk about anger at my house? I suspect that it was a variety of reasons: my parents and the children didn't know how anger works, we didn't know what to do with it, we were afraid of it getting worse and somebody getting hurt.

It's important for us to understand what anger is, how it works, why God has given it to us, and how we are to express it.

There are some basics about anger that will help us as we discuss it later. We need to understand at least three basic things: anger is secondary, anger is neutral, and anger is powerful. I teach college. These are the fundamentals if I were to introduce the course Anger 101.

ANGER IS SECONDARY

Anger might arise from something so simple as overwork, stress, lack of sleep, or inadequate relaxation. But mostly anger happens as a result of some other emotionally painful event, thought, or relationship. Behind the feeling of anger is something else. Anger is secondary to some other root cause.

Think back to the example in chapter 2: Someone carelessly cuts us off in heavy traffic. For many of us, this would lead to anger. But what happens first is a sense that I have been endangered, disrespected, or insulted. The other driver has failed to respect my need for safety. Or, if I do not feel insulted, I may be afraid because I quickly imagined I would be in a horrible crash. But the cause of this fear is someone else's action. A careless driver threatened my safety. It's *his* fault. So we end up in the same place: we are angry.

In another example, you find out that the teacher has exposed your sixth-grade child to inappropriate material at school. Maybe it was a story he had to read or a movie she had to watch. You are uncharacteristically upset. Where does this come from? Love for your son or hurt over your daughter facing potential danger.

We see this secondary nature of anger in Mark 3:5. The anger of Jesus arises from grief. His grief arises from seeing Pharisees so hard-hearted that they refuse to allow healing on the Sabbath. This episode also tells us that not all anger is sinful (more on this later).

ANGER IS NEUTRAL

Anger is neutral. By neutral, I mean that some anger is good and some is bad; some is righteous and some unrighteous. We saw the same thing with joy (chapter 3): some joy is based in truth. So Paul urges us to rejoice in the Lord (Philippians 4:4). Some joy, however, is based in sin. So in 1 Corinthians 13:6, Paul basically forbids us to rejoice at wrongdoing. Likewise, anger in itself is neutral—the feeling, the mere "being angry"—but some causes for anger, and some ways of showing it, might be wrong; others might be right. We can place anger into two categories: unrighteous (wrongful) and righteous (proper) anger.

Here are a few examples of *unrighteous anger*:

Second Kings 5:1–8 tells how Naaman, the commander of Syria's army, sought a cure for his leprosy. When Naaman heard from an Israelite girl that the prophet Elisha could cure the illness, he sought Elijah's help. The prophet sent a messenger to him, saying, "Go and wash in the Jordan seven times, and your flesh shall be restored, and you shall be clean" (v. 10).

Instead of obeying the instruction, Naaman became angry and went away, saying, " 'Behold, I thought that he would surely come out to me and stand and call upon the name of the Lord his God, and wave his hand over the place and cure the leper. Are not Abana and Pharpar, the rivers of Damascus, better than all the waters of Israel? Could I not wash in them and be clean?' So he turned and went away in a rage" (vv. 11–12). Considering himself an important man of power, he expected the respect of a face-to-face encounter with Elijah, and welled up in anger. This was unjustified anger, based on pride. When he relented and obeyed, he was cured (vv. 13–14).

Matthew 2:1–16 recounts the magi from the east looking for one "born king of the Jews" and Herod's response. King Herod was "troubled, and in a deceptive request, asks the magi to pass on to him the location of this babe so that "I too may come and worship him" (vv. 7–8). But they do no such thing and the king is incensed. "Herod, when he saw that he had been tricked by the wise men, became furious, and he sent and killed all the male children in Bethlehem and in all that region who were two years old or under, according to the time that he had ascertained from the wise men" (v. 16).

Herod's anger is morally wrong and yet completely rational. It is wrong in that it arises from his arrogance, fearfulness, selfishness, and his rejection of God. It is completely rational in that it fits his character, beliefs, and the mechanism of anger we discussed earlier: Someone is threatening a thing important to him (his power). Someone has tricked him (an insult to his honor).

Such anger is out of control and even vindictive. Unlike the godly person who "has distributed freely [and] given to the poor . . . The wicked man sees it and is angry; he gnashes his teeth and melts away" (Psalm 112:9–10).

Let's look at some biblical examples of righteous anger. Moses has been on the mountain with God. While there, the people grow impatient and make a god for themselves, a golden calf (Exodus 32:1–6). Moses cannot see what is going on in the camp of Israel, but the Lord can, and He warns Moses that such rebellion threatens to bring God's wrath, which would destroy the whole nation (vv. 7–10). Moses intercedes and the people as a whole are spared (vv. 11–14).

> Then Moses turned and went down from the mountain with the two tablets of the testimony in his hand, tablets that were written on both sides. . . . The tablets were the work of God, and the writing was the writing of God, engraved on the tablets. . . . And as soon as he came near the camp and saw the calf and the dancing, Moses' anger burned hot, and he threw the tablets out of his hands and broke them at the foot of the mountain. (vv. 15–16, 19)

The reaction of Moses is completely appropriate; he is feeling the displeasure that the Lord felt. Both Moses and the Lord have been betrayed, for the people had previously been commanded to worship only Yahweh (Exodus 20:1–5) and they had promised to do so (24:3, 7). What follows is a series of actions, all motivated by Moses' godly anger:

- *The destruction of the idol.* "He took the calf that they had made and burned it with fire and ground it to powder and scattered it on the water and made the people of Israel drink it" (v. 20).
- *The rebuke of the leadership.* "And Moses said to Aaron, 'What did this people do to you that you have brought such a great sin upon them?'" (v. 21).
- *The punishment of the idolaters.* The Levites killed about three thousand men (vv. 25–28).

We could easily be tempted to think that, even if anger is at times allowed, it is always second best. But the emotions of Jesus are never second best. And at various times Jesus displayed a righteous anger.

Mark says that some people from the crowds "were bringing children to him that he might touch them." Apparently the disciples thought children were not important or that the gospel was beyond them, so the disciples rebuked those bringing their children to the Master. When Jesus saw this He became angry. The precise term is "indignant," a type of anger that arises when one encounters injustice or moral wrong (see Mark 10:41, 14:4). This event is also presented in Matthew 19:13–15 and Luke 18:15–17 as well, and both Matthew and Luke add that Jesus placed His hands on the children.

JESUS SHOWED His anger over disrespect for "my Father's house" when He chased the vendors from the temple courts.

Both Mark and Luke describe Jesus' rebuke of the disciples for trying to keep the children from Him. Jesus became angry when He saw the children being treated poorly. And to make His love for the children clear, Jesus blessed the children as they sat in His arms (Mark 10:16).

This event was not isolated. As we saw earlier, Jesus was angry with hard-hearted Pharisees in Mark 3:5. In addition, He cleansed the temple, driving out the sellers and money changers (John 2:13–16); in His anger He made a whip of cords and snapped it at them and tossed their tables aside. This was an angry action—controlled, righteous, but angry nonetheless. He showed His anger over such disrespect for "my Father's house" at the end of His ministry as well, when once again He chased the vendors from the temple courts, overturning their tables in the process (Matthew 21:8–13; cf. John 2:16).

ANGER IS POWERFUL

We feel the physiological results of anger like no other emotion. The much-visited Internet site www.webmd.com summarizes this well: "Anger signals your body to prepare for a fight. This reaction is commonly classified as 'fight or flight.' When you get angry, adrenaline and other hormones are released into the bloodstream, then your blood pressure goes up, your heart beats faster, and you breathe faster."[2]

The power of anger is one of the reasons Scripture gives so many warnings against it. Anger can be very destructive. Jesus told those listening, "You have heard that it was said to those of old, 'You shall not murder; and whoever murders will be liable to judgment.' But I say to you that everyone who is angry with his brother will be liable to judgment; whoever insults his brother will be liable to the council; and whoever says, 'You fool!' will be liable to the hell of fire" (Matthew 5:21–22).

Paul admonished the Ephesian church, "Let all bitterness and wrath and anger and clamor and slander be put away from you, along with all malice. Be kind to one another, tenderhearted, forgiving one another, as God in Christ forgave you" (Ephesians 4:31–32). There is a kind of anger that endures, breeds bitterness, and so stifles real Christian community.

WHY GOD GAVE US ANGER

With such consequence, we wonder if it's worth having anger. But as the website web.com notes, anger prepares us for action—to fight (or sometimes to flee). But when we're ready to fight, we have the energy to undertake vigorous, righteous action—action to right wrongs, action to protect the weak, action to accomplish things that are important to us. When angry, we find that we have more courage and motivation than when we are not angry. The physiological changes in our body prepare us to do something.

A particularly good example comes from Nehemiah 5:1–10. Many Israelites have returned from exile in Babylon and are trying to reestablish themselves in Jerusalem. Nehemiah is serving as their governor. But a complaint arises from the poorer Jews against the wealthier: the poor have been suffering economic hardship to the point of selling their children! The passage says:

> Now there arose a great outcry of the people and of their wives against their Jewish brothers. For there were those who said, "With our sons and our daughters, we are many. So let us get grain, that we may eat and keep alive." There were also those who said, "We are mortgaging our fields, our vineyards, and our houses to get grain because of the famine." And there were those who said, "We have borrowed money for the king's tax on our fields and our vineyards. Now our flesh is as the flesh of our brothers, our children are as their children. Yet we are forcing our sons and our daughters to be slaves, and some of our daughters have already been enslaved, but it is not in our power to help it, for other men have our fields and our vineyards."
>
> I was very angry when I heard their outcry and these

words. I took counsel with myself, and I brought charges against the nobles and the officials. I said to them, "You are exacting interest, each from his brother." And I held a great assembly against them and said to them, "We, as far as we are able, have bought back our Jewish brothers who have been sold to the nations, but you even sell your brothers that they may be sold to us!" They were silent and could not find a word to say. So I said, "The thing that you are doing is not good. Ought you not to walk in the fear of our God to prevent the taunts of the nations our enemies? Moreover, I and my brothers and my servants are lending them money and grain. Let us abandon this exacting of interest."

This is anger against injustice. The injustice has come about through disobedience to the Law of Moses (charging interest; see Exodus 22:25; Deuteronomy 23:19). Thankfully Nehemiah was angry; the anger gave the courage and motivation needed to confront leaders in the community.

THE SUM OF OUR FEELINGS

Anger is hard for us to deal with; typically we are scared to talk about it. But we should be talking about it since God invites the conversation. The first time human anger is mentioned in the Bible, the Lord asks Cain, "Why are you angry?" It's a question we should ask ourselves.

Since Jesus Himself became angry (Mark 3:5), we know that not all anger is wrong. There are, however, three important things to know about anger. First, anger is secondary; it arises because of some other emotionally painful event, thought, or relationship. Anger can arise from the pain of an insult, or from the pain

of a goal that wasn't reached. Second, anger is not always bad—
some anger is good and some is bad; some anger is righteous and
some unrighteous. Only an examination of the situation and our
own hearts can discern the difference. Third, anger is powerful.
We feel the physiological results of anger like no other emotion:
the adrenaline rush, tense muscles, increased heart rate, aggres-
sive feelings and actions.

We often express our anger improperly, and there are many
examples of inappropriate anger in Scripture (e.g., Genesis 49:5–
7; Numbers 22:27; 1 Samuel 20:30; Luke 15:28). Nevertheless,
when used properly, anger can be a powerful tool to motivate us
to action against injustice and wrong.

Toward a Healthy Emotional Life

To have a healthy emotional life, our use of anger must be measured and appropriate—avoiding unrighteous anger while cultivating righteous anger. Let's look first at *how to avoid unrighteous anger.*

When it comes to avoiding unrighteous anger, remember that God, in His grace, is willing to enter into conversation with people who are angry. His questions about anger (in Genesis 4) should be our questions about anger.

1. *Read Genesis 4:1–7,* the account of Cain's anger toward his brother Abel. This is the first instance of human anger in Scripture. Rather than an outburst of wrath or condemnation, God initiates a conversation with Cain by asking, "Why are you angry?" *So ask yourself the same question: Why am I angry?* Our evil motivations are often hidden from us until we begin to explore what is going on in our hearts and minds.

2. *Engage in diligent prayer and request the gentle help of others* who know you well to answer these questions:

   a. Does my anger come from a desire to be seen as powerful or competent, or a desire to be honored by others? If so, I will be easily insulted.

   b. Does my anger come from a desire to avoid fearful or embarrassing situations by controlling people and things? If so, I will tend to manipulate people and insist on my own way.

   c. Does my anger come from a desire to obtain justice for myself now, rather than patiently waiting? If so, I am not viewing myself as a forgiven sinner, but as a judge.

    d. Does my anger come from a desire to accomplish per-
    sonal goals at the expense of others? If so, my own pride
    (accomplishments) has become more important than
    love (serving others, seeking their goals).

3. *Meditate on key Bible passages.* Typically what is at stake in
our anger is our own sense of being secure, being competent, and being right. Allender and Longman state it well: "If
the essence of righteous anger is a hatred of sin and a love of
beauty, then the core of unrighteous anger is a hatred of vulnerability and a love of control."[3] In all too many cases, such
hatred and love arise from seeking security and love in the
self and not in the gospel. If this is true, then one way to have
less anger is to find greater security, safety. I suggest pondering, believing, and praying over such passages as these two:
Ephesians 3:14–19 and Romans 8:31–39.

4. *Cultivate the righteous kind of anger.* Righteous anger can
exist, as Moses, Jesus, and Paul demonstrate. If Jesus is our
model, then our goal during this life must not be anger-free,
but to have a godly manifestation of all emotions, anger included. To help you develop and recognize righteous anger
in your own life, ask these questions and make the following
outcomes your goals:

    a. Does my anger come from a desire to see the justice of
    God ruling in the world? If so, I will be grieved when the
    poor and weak are exploited.
    b. Does my anger come from a concern for the truths of
    the gospel or from a zeal for things of God? If so, I will do
    what is appropriate to hold Christian leaders accountable.

    c. Does my anger come from a desire to see the security and well-being of those close to me? If so, I will feel threatened when they suffer.

5. *Use your righteous anger as a motivator for appropriate action.* For example, you could turn your anger about human trafficking into support for the International Justice Mission or another compassion or social justice ministry. You or I could turn our anger over our spouse's irresponsibility into thoughtful confrontation and a mutually-agreeable plan for change.

    In all cases, be willing to risk your comfort for others. When you and I do that, we are imitating the righteous anger and genuine love of Jesus.

    But what about anger *with* God? Do we treat it the same way? We will answer those questions in our next chapter.

Questions for Discussion

1. Describe how anger was handled and expressed in your family while growing up. Tell how those early years either help you or hinder you in the present.
2. Discuss what it means for anger to be a "secondary" emotion. How does this understanding help us to deal properly with our anger?
3. Do you agree or disagree and tell why: "God gave us anger because it prepares us for action."
4. Ponder your last episode of unrighteous anger and ask the following questions of it:
   a. Did my anger come from a desire to be seen as powerful or competent, or a desire to be honored by others?
   b. Did my anger come from a desire to avoid fearful or embarrassing situations by controlling people and things?
   c. Did my anger come from a desire to obtain justice for myself now, rather than patiently waiting?
   d. Did my anger come from a desire to accomplish personal goals at the expense of others?
5. Ephesians 4:31–32 seems to prohibit all anger. On the other hand Ephesians 4:26 commands anger. How should we reconcile these two?

Suggestions for Further Reading

Allender, Dan and Tremper Longman III. *The Cry of the Soul: How Our Emotions Reveal Our Deepest Questions about God.* (Colorado Springs: NavPress, 1994.

Rosberg, Gary. *Dr. Rosberg's Do-It-Yourself Relationship Mender.* Colorado Springs, Focus on the Family, 1995.

6 ◆ What If I'm Angry *with* God?

I HAVE OFTEN HEARD Christians talk about anger toward God as if it were just one step away from abandoning faith. And, of course, such conversations are scary for us. Many believers are quite afraid of expressing such emotion toward God. What if He is angry with us in return?

Some recall what happened when the descendants of Korah rose up and rebelled against Moses: "The earth opened its mouth and swallowed them up, with their households and all the people who belonged to Korah and all their goods" (Numbers 16:32).

Uzzah wasn't angry with God; he just tried to be helpful. Second Samuel 6:6–7 records that as the ark of the covenant was being transported, when it "came to the threshing floor of Nacon, Uzzah put out his hand to the ark of God and took hold of it, for the oxen stumbled. And the anger of the Lord was kindled against Uzzah, and God struck him down there because of his error, and he died there beside the ark of God." Uzzah was not a Levite—not part of the priesthood, and not authorized to transport (nor touch) the ark.

And lest we forget—many of us remember quite well the first time we read these verses in Acts 5:1–5—Ananias and Sapphira died on the spot because they lied to God.

Such events might make us very hesitant to admit we have anger toward God or to express anger toward God. Likewise, if a brother or sister in Christ is angry with God, most of us are paralyzed. What are we supposed to do?

First, let's recall one truth about anger we considered in chapter 5. We know that anger is secondary. Behind the feeling of anger is something else. Anger arises from some painful incident. There is a corollary to this truth: We are more easily hurt by those close to us. We are easily hurt by a spouse, not by someone who passes into and out of our life for a season. We are more easily hurt by our own parents than by the parents of a complete stranger. From this it follows that being close to God is no guarantee that we will never be angry with Him. If we have known God for some time and believe He exists and is an active force, we can easily become angry with God, especially if evil seems to flourish and the godly seem to be powerless (Psalms 74:10–11, 94:1–5).

THE DIFFERENCES BETWEEN BEING ANGRY *WITH* AND ANGRY *ABOUT* GOD

There is a difference between being angry *with* and angry *about*: Typically we are angry *with* someone *about* something. So we are angry *with* our boss *about* the fact that working conditions are so bad. We are angry *with* our spouse *about* an insulting comment he or she made. We are angry *with* our child *about* a disrespectful attitude.

If a person is angry with God, he or she can rightfully ask: *What am I angry about?* There are lots of possibilities. He could be angry about a painful, long-term illness. Day after day, week after week, dealing with the pain and disability becomes emotionally exhausting. But God does not heal. Why? She could become angry with God about relationships. A wife is betrayed by her husband. Even though she put massive amounts of time and energy into the relationship, he has broken his vows. Why didn't God stop this betrayal? Or perhaps the anger is about children who have rebelled and brought heartache to both parents. They become angry about noble goals they had for their children: a certain job, family, fulfillment. It does not happen. The disappointment grows and God is questioned: Why don't You give me this thing I long for? It's not evil.

Discerning what a person is angry about is easier. A different and more difficult question is, Why do people become angry *with God*? If a spouse betrays, or an illness lasts, or a child rebels, why not just be angry with the spouse, with the illness, or with the child? I suggest that people can only become angry with God if they have good theology. That is, they believe certain orthodox things about God:

- *God is all-knowing* (omniscient). He knows all about the pain in our life. We will not become angry with God if we think that He is ignorant of what is going on with us.
- *God is all-powerful* (omnipotent). He is capable of doing whatever He wants to do. He could bring a change. We will not become angry with God if we think that He does not have the power to stop our suffering.
- *God is active.* He is not sitting back passively but is working in the lives of people. We will not become angry with God if we think that He does not act in His world.
- *God is all good* (omnibenevolent). He wants to bless, to save, to cherish. We will not become angry with God if we think that He is evil and has no desire to stop our suffering.

God *is* omniscient, omnipotent, always benevolent, and active in the world. It *is* good and right for us to believe these things about Him. The problem comes with making sense of our pain and our life's challenges in light of these four truths. And it is not just any pain. There is plenty of pain around the world that might not lead us to be angry with God. It is *personal* pain, intense pain that hits close to home, pain that threatens our sense of well-being. We expected God to protect us from a family member's abuse, but it went on for several years anyway. *Where is God?*

My son should take care of me when I am old but a traumatic brain injury means I will take care of him for the rest of my life. What is God doing?

For a husband and wife, it may be waiting and waiting for a child. *We had hoped for a big family, but what seems like thousands of doctor visits has not found a solution to our infertility. Does God care?*

In these cases—and many more like them—we might find it hard to make sense of a good, all-powerful, active, and all-knowing God allowing such pain to continue in our lives.

ONE PERSPECTIVE: "BEING ANGRY WITH GOD IS NEVER RIGHT"

How should we regard any anger we feel toward God? Some Bible experts believe such anger is at best arrogance and at worst just a step away from apostasy. From this perspective, to be angry with God is to stop trusting Him, and instead to become God's judge. And this is a dangerous place to be. John Piper expresses this view, writing:

> What is anger? The common definition is: "An intense emotional state induced by displeasure" (Merriam-Webster). But there is an ambiguity in this definition. You can be "displeased" by a thing or by a person.

Anger at a thing does not contain indignation at a choice or an act. We simply don't like the effect of the thing: the broken clutch, or the grain of sand that just blew in our eye, or rain on our picnic. But when we get angry at a person, we are displeased with a choice they made and an act they performed. Anger at a person always implies strong disapproval. If you are angry at me, you think I have done something I should not have done.

This is why being angry at God is never right. It is wrong—always wrong—to disapprove of God for what he does and permits. "Shall not the Judge of all the earth do what is just?" (Genesis 18:25). It is arrogant for finite, sinful creatures to disapprove of God for what he does and permits. We may weep over the pain. We may be angry at sin and Satan. But God does only what is right.[1]

If this is the perspective we take on anger with God, we might live with all sorts of guilt and shame about our anger with God. We might separate ourselves from other Christians because we are afraid they will judge us harshly for our anger. We might work hard on suppressing our anger or on trying to not be angry—a futile exercise.

Even though John Piper's view is logical, it is not the perspective on anger with God that we see worked out in Scripture. As always, we need to look at some scriptural examples to understand God's perspective on our anger with Him.

THE BIBLICAL PERSPECTIVE SHOWN BY JOB, NAOMI, JEREMIAH, AND JONAH

The Bible presents four major characters who are angry with God. In all cases they declare their negative emotions in a complaint expressed to God or expressed about God. We will call this complaining to/about God a "lament." Whether or not we agree on anger with God being right or wrong, it is beyond dispute that many in Scripture express such lament.

Job is direct in his complaint. He declares to his three companions his feelings of bitterness:

> I loathe my life; I will give free utterance to my complaint; I will speak in the bitterness of my soul. I will say to God: Do not condemn me; let me know why you contend against me. Does it seem good to you to oppress, to despise the work of your hands and favor the designs of the wicked?" (Job 10:1–3)

Job's situation is familiar yet vast in scope. He suffered the loss of children, of property, of health, of social prestige, even of his wife's support (Job 1:9). His comforters only accuse him of sin, even though God's verdict is that Job is righteous (1:10, 2:3). Job's words in 10:1–3 are similar to earlier verses:

> Job 7:11: "I will complain in the bitterness of my soul."
> Job 9:18: "[God] will not let me get my breath, but fills me with bitterness."
> Job 9:21: "I am blameless; I regard not myself; I loathe my life."
> Job 9:27–28: "If I say, 'I will forget my complaint, I will put off my sad face, and be of good cheer,' I become afraid of all my suffering, for I know you will not hold me innocent."

In Job 10 the bitter Job is complaining to God, accusing God of unrighteousness: from what Job can see, God unjustly favors the wicked and does not favor the godly. And it is not only against Job himself, but Job mentions God's favor toward the wicked. That is, it is no longer just his situation. Similarly in 24:1–2, Job will refer to the plight of the poor, widows, and children. *His own agonies bring him to complain about all injustice on earth.*

Clearly Job is angry. We don't need to see the words "Job was angry and said . . ." We can see the anger from what Job says and from how he says it. We can also see anger in the sarcasm of verse 3: "Does it seem good to you to oppress?" Sarcasm, as should be well known, is most often attached to anger.

BEWILDERMENT, anguish, physical pain, embarrassment, grief, and depression can all exist with anger.

This is not to say that anger is Job's only emotion. As we keep mentioning, anger is secondary. Bewilderment, anguish, physical pain, embarrassment, grief, and depression, can all exist in and with the anger.

Why is Job angry with God? As we said earlier, in part it is because Job has a good theology. He believes that God is in control of the world (12:14–25), that God knows all that is going on in creation (28:23–27, 36:27–33), and that God is wise and benevolent (5:15–16, 9:4, 12:13). But at this point, while he is enduring such loss and disease, Job does not see the benevolent control of God in his own life. To whom shall he go with these feelings? He confides with friends, yes. But he also talks with God, expressing his feelings of confusion, anger, and even bitterness.

Consider *Naomi*. Due to a famine in their land, Naomi, with her husband and two sons, leave Bethlehem to reside in Moab. Sadly, while there her husband and two sons die (Ruth 1:5), leaving her with only two daughters-in-law (v. 7), who, to make matters worse, are Moabites, not of her faith. Hearing that food is again growing in Israel, she returns to her land with Ruth, one of her daughters-in law, who wanted to join Naomi's people (vv. 6–7, 16–18).

When she arrives back in Bethlehem, "the whole town was stirred because of them. And the women said, 'Is this Naomi?' She said to them, 'Do not call me Naomi; call me Mara, for the Almighty has dealt very bitterly with me. I went away full, and the Lord has brought me back empty. Why call me Naomi, when the Lord has testified against me and the Almighty has brought calamity upon me?'" (vv. 19–21).

As with Job, so also with Naomi bitterness has to do with anger. And also like Job, she views God as the cause of her problems. There is no hint of the idea that God is distant, powerless, uninvolved. She expresses her pain freely—and there is no rebuke from God.

Jeremiah the prophet receives a difficult ministry. During this time in Israel many had turned their backs on God and were worshiping idols. God calls Jeremiah to the difficult task of rebuking God's people for their sins. The Lord says, "I will declare my judgments against them, for all their evil in forsaking me. They have made offerings to other gods and worshiped the works of their own hands" (Jeremiah 1:16). This is not a message that many will welcome.

One who opposes the message from God via Jeremiah is the priest Pashhur, the chief officer in the house of the Lord. After he hears Jeremiah's prophecy, Pashhur beats Jeremiah "and [puts] him in the stocks" (20:1–2). Unfazed, the faithful Jeremiah the next day delivers a harsh rebuke against Pashhur. But Jeremiah's courage does not last long. Soon the pain, shame, and defeat get to him. Later in chapter 20 we read:

> O Lord, you have deceived me, and I was deceived; you are stronger than I, and you have prevailed. I have become a laughingstock all the day; everyone mocks me. For whenever I speak, I cry out, I shout, "Violence and destruction!" For the word of the Lord has become for me a reproach and derision all day long. If I say, "I will not mention him, or speak any more in his name," there is in my heart as it were a burning fire shut up in my bones, and I am weary with holding it in, and I cannot. For I hear many whispering. Terror is on every side! "Denounce him! Let us denounce him!" say all my close friends, watching for my fall. . . . Cursed be the day on which I was born! The day when my mother bore me, let it not be blessed! Cursed be the man who brought the news to my father, "A son is born to you," making him very glad. . . . Why did I come out from the womb to see toil and sorrow, and spend my days in shame? (20:7–18)

Clearly Jeremiah is in deep pain. In this passage we see a prophet suffering public humiliation through mockery (v. 7), ridicule (v. 7), scorn (v. 8), and derision (v. 8). Regarding God, Jeremiah complains of feeling bullied ("deceived," v. 7). Although he tries to resist God's call to be a prophet (Jeremiah 1:6–7), Yahweh will have nothing of it. Jeremiah seems disappointed with how God is working (see 12:1–2, 15:15–18). And so, as often seems to be the case with us, Jeremiah's only hope has become his biggest problem. God's sovereign power has brought on his suffering and paradoxically and perhaps even perplexingly, is also the only guarantee of his ultimate vindication.[2]

Jeremiah writes a Hebrew poem (vv. 7–18) in which he blames Yahweh for Jeremiah's inability to keep the word to himself. Jeremiah is tired of holding it in. He feels isolated, friendless, trapped. Everywhere he hears derision. All his close friends hope for his downfall. He has no way out.

JEREMIAH FEELS isolated, friendless, trapped. His only option is to take this pain to God; and he does just that.

His only option is to take this pain to God; and he does just that. But could you imagine speaking to God the way that Jeremiah does?! As He has with Job and Naomi, God allows Jeremiah's lament, a reflection of his anger, without punishing the angry prophet in his complaint.

Then there's *Jonah,* a prophet who becomes angry when his message *is* accepted. The repentance of the wicked people of Nineveh "displeased Jonah exceedingly, and he was angry" (Jonah 4:1). Why would the prophet Jonah be upset that the people obey his warning and repent? Basically, because he believes the people are undeserving of forgiveness. In an "I told you so" prayer, Jonah rebukes God:

> "O Lord, is not this what I said when I was yet in my country? That is why I made haste to flee to Tarshish; for I knew that you are a gracious God and merciful, slow to anger and abounding in steadfast love, and relenting

from disaster. Therefore now, O Lord, please take my life from me, for it is better for me to die than to live." And the Lord said, "Do you do well to be angry?" (4:1–4).

Jonah's theology is right; God is indeed gracious, merciful, slow to anger, and abounding in steadfast love. It is because Jonah believes these things that he has a problem. He becomes resentful and depressed. And God responds directly, not with a rebuke but with a question.

LAMENT—THE WAY TO RESOLVE ANGER WITH GOD

These four character studies are just a few examples of how godly people responded to situations that evoked anger toward God. Many other examples could be drawn from the Psalms, for the largest category of psalms is not psalms that praise God, but psalms of lament (e.g., Psalms 12, 44, 60, 74, 79, 80, 83, 85, 90, 94, 123, 126, 129).

There is no indication that God despises or rejects our complaint when we are angry with Him. Instead Scripture sanctions lament as the way that such anger is resolved. And anger must be resolved, because unresolved anger leads to estrangement in the relationship. "Unresolved anger in any relationship, as we learn from counseling with couples and families," writes Andrew D. Lester in the *Journal of Pastoral Theology,* "creates silence, emotional withdrawal, a feeling of distance and disconnection, even alienation."[3]

IS ANGER TOWARD GOD A SIN?

So we return to the question of whether anger with God is a sin. But it is not a helpful question since the Bible does not address the question that way. In any case, it never explicitly calls such anger a sin. Further, there is no indication that anger is resolved by denying it or trying to shut it off. That avenue is a dead end that leads to alienation. On the other hand, laments by individuals are common in Scripture. What is lament?

We can define lament as a painful prayer to God for help or a complaint to God regarding pain, evil, social injustice, or sin. The prayer and the complaint elements might be mixed; the words might be brief or extended. Laments can contain "expressions of grief, sorrow, fear, anger, contempt, shame, guilt, and other dark emotions."[4]

The person expressing lament goes to God and communicates these painful emotions to Him, because, in the final analysis, only God can completely understand, only God can change what seems impossible, only God can help. As we lament, we wait, not necessarily for God to answer, but for His assurance of care and wisdom. And soon our anger can abate as we return to trust Him.

At the end of such honesty in our communication, each lament holds the hope of restoration with God. We can illustrate it this way:

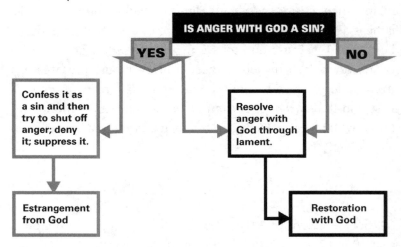

Scripture deals with the right path; indeed, this is the only path Scripture gives us. It does not go down the left path. So no matter how we answer the question, we have only one option. We must bring our anger with God to God. When we do, when we resolve our anger with God through lament—honest communication that awaits His comfort (and sometimes His answer, though His explanation need not come to find His comfort)—there is restoration with God.

THE SUM OF OUR FEELINGS

To ask if anger with God is a sin is to ask a yes-or-no question. Such a question is like trying to solve a complex mathematical problem. If we put ourselves and God into a *relationship* instead of putting God and ourselves into a *mathematical equation*, we will draw this conclusion: The God who is willing to die for the sins of His enemies (Romans 5:10) is willing to listen to the lament of His beloved people (Psalm 60:1–5).

Since Scripture often uses the analogy of marriage, we could think of it this way: A husband and wife must sometimes engage each other in argument that is motivated by anger (i.e., one or both feels wronged). Yet because they have agreed to a marriage covenant, there is no threat of divorce; no threat of abandonment. Instead the goal is reconciliation. The conversation is painful but honest and transparent.

So also, while still being firmly committed to the covenant relationship, a Christian might become angry with God and engage Him in a conversation. There is no threat of apostasy; no threat of abandonment. Instead the goal is reconciliation. As with the examples of Job, Naomi, and Jonah the conversation is painful but honest and transparent.

Toward a Healthy Emotional Life

1. *Review and observe the guidelines in the last chapter* for discerning where anger comes from. Bring these motivations before God.

2. *Bring your complaints to God,* just as Job, Naomi, Jeremiah, and Jonah did. Consider writing in a journal all the reasons for your anger. Examine each reason in light of the cross.

3. *What areas of your life have brought blessing or joy? Write them down in a journal.* Typically, when we are angry with God, we are not angry about everything, but only particular events or losses that we can't figure out.

4. After you have read chapter 9 on contentment and holy longing, *follow its guidelines in order to temper your anger with God* in one area with your thankfulness to Him in another.

5. *Read through a lament Psalm* (such as 44) and use it to help you understand your mind and emotions and to verbalize what is happening. Search for ways the Psalm writer resolves the anger. Can you resolve yours the same way?

6. *Find a like-minded friend who can help in the journey toward resolution.* This is not a process that needs to happen alone. The Psalms were Israel's hymnbook and thus the lament Psalms were sung by groups of people.

Questions for Discussion

1. In your view, is anger with God right or wrong? Explain your answer. For either answer (yes or no), tell how the answer affects what you can say to God in prayer.
2. The author says, "People can only become angry with God if they have good theology." Do you agree or disagree? Explain.
3. What's the difference between *angry with* and *angry about*?
4. What have you typically done with your anger toward God? Would you say that this has been a helpful or unhelpful strategy?
5. Read through Psalm 44 and discuss how the writer resolves anger with God.
6. I heard a Christian friend say, "My church often sings songs taken from the happy Psalms but never a song from the lament Psalms." Has this been your experience? Discuss.

Suggestions for Further Reading

Chapman, Gary. "When You Are Angry at God," in *Anger: Handling a Powerful Emotion in a Healthy Way*. Chicago: Northfield, 2007.

Lester, Andrew D. *The Angry Christian: A Theology for Care and Counseling*. Louisville: John Knox Press, 2003.

7 ◆ Is *Love* Only An Action?

OUR CULTURE HAS a pretty weak view of love. According to the movies, television, and your average celebrity, love is fickle, selfish, misinformed, and based on emotion alone. Too often I've heard a man say about his marriage, "We're not in love anymore." By this he means that romantic feelings are gone. Apparently he thinks that these feelings are like a match—it's hot once but can't be struck again!

Such a view of love is sad; of course, it needs to be corrected. It would be going to another extreme, however, for us to conclude that love is only action and has no emotional content. But in fact, this is where many Christians are; it's a view being taught by many well-respected teachers. For example, one well-known contributor to the *Daily Scripture Blog* says,

> Love is more than attraction and more than arousal. It's also more than sentimentality, like so many of today's songs suggest. By this standard, is love dead when the emotion is gone? No, not at all. Because love is an action; love is a behavior.
>
> Over and over again, in the Bible, God commands us to love each other. And you can't command an emotion. If I told you "Be sad!" right now, you couldn't be sad on cue. Just like an actor, you can fake it, but you're not wired for your emotions to change on command. Have you ever told a little kid, "Be happy!" I'm trying, Daddy!
>
> If love were just an emotion, then God couldn't

command it. But love is something you do. It can produce emotion, but love is an action.[1]

The view that love is only action does have its advantages.
First, it steers us away from a secular view that almost wholly
defines love as a feeling, especially romantic love. So we hear, "I
don't love him/her anymore." That is, romantic feelings are gone.
Second, it rightly draws our attention to the necessity of love being displayed in proper action. So please don't misunderstand
what I'm saying: *Love should be demonstrated in proper action.*

FOUR FLAWS IN THE "LOVE IS ACTION" APPROACH

On the other hand, this view has disadvantages. First, it leads
to a pharisaic approach to what God wants from us, an approach
that says serving God is an issue of the body and not an issue of
the heart. The love-is-action approach says, "God is looking for
us to do something. It does not matter what emotion we have
behind it." Jesus, however, spoke out strongly against such a perspective. For example, in Matthew 6:1–2 He said, "Beware of
practicing your righteousness before other people in order to be
seen by them, for then you will have no reward from your Father
who is in heaven. Thus, when you give to the needy, sound no
trumpet before you, as the hypocrites do in the synagogues and
in the streets, that they may be praised by others. Truly, I say to
you, they have received their reward."

According to Jesus, a good action (giving to the needy) with
a wrong motivation (desire to be seen as godly) is not love. It's
hypocrisy. We know that such actions are not godly actions because they receive no reward from God.

Second, this approach to love is actually contrary to how we ourselves want to be treated. We typically do not want action without proper emotion. Remember the man in chapter 1 who gave his wife flowers out of a sense of duty. Even though the action was a good action, in her view it was not acceptable because of its motivation. It wasn't a loving motivation. If you doubt this, you're probably a bachelor, and your error will be corrected when you get married.

Third, let's think about this the other way around. We often set up hate as the opposite emotion to love. Applying the love-is-action view to hatred, we would say: "Hate is only an action. I only hate a person if I act toward him or her in a certain way." This perspective is obviously wrong; we can harbor hatred in our hearts for someone while we try to give the impression we are actually kind and loving.

Fourth, the love-is-action approach makes nonsense of many common interactions in our life. Take, for instance, the godly Christian wife who says to her husband, "I love you." What does this statement mean? Is the husband really supposed to understand that she is saying, "I act toward you in a certain way"? Obviously not! Her comment speaks of her inner world; it reveals the esteem, the affection, the particular emotion she has toward him.

So we understand the comment "I love you" well enough. But for some odd reason when we come to talk about what love is, we draw the obviously wrong conclusion that love is only action.

LOVE AS A MOTIVATOR FOR ACTION

While Scripture certainly makes plain that there is a strong connection between love and action, it does not present love as only an action. Rather, it regularly presents love as a motivation or cause for an action. Love is an emotion that has to do with the perceived worth of something; we put a positive emotion onto what we consider valuable. Dozens of examples from the Scriptures could be given. Here are just seven.

2 Chronicles 2:11: King David had diplomatic relations with Hiram, king of Tyre. So when Solomon, David's son, planned to build a temple for the Lord, he reaffirmed the diplomatic relation and sent word to Hiram asking for aid. In response, Hiram wrote, "Because the Lord loves his people, he has made you king over them." Let's read this from the perspective of the "love-is-action" view. It says, "Because God acts a certain way, He acts a certain way." This reading runs contrary to normal understanding of language. The passage gives love as a cause for action. God values His people, therefore He blesses them with a wise king.

Psalm 52:3 speaks directly to a wicked man and says, "You love evil more than good, and lying more than speaking what is right." That is, the wicked man has no affection for or pleasure in goodness and righteousness; he loves the opposite. "'Love' here means to prefer or to take pleasure in something (cf. Psalms 11:5, 7; 109:17; Proverbs 20:13, 21:17; etc.)."[2] So love is primarily considered a disposition or emotion.

Proverbs 27:5 advises, "Better is open rebuke than hidden love." Of course, if love is only action, it cannot be hidden. But if love is primarily an emotion or motivation, then the unfortunate truth is that it can be hidden.

Luke 11:43 has strong words from Jesus to the religious leaders: "Woe to you Pharisees! For you love the first seat in the synagogues and greetings in the marketplace." Does the verse only mean that they selected the best seats? If you observe over the course of weeks or months that a man always selected a certain seat, what conclusion would you draw? Would you only conclude that he always selected a certain seat? Or would you conclude that he likes—dare I say it, loves—a certain seat the best and therefore selects it? Why love the best seats? They are valuable because they bring social esteem to those who sit in them.

John 14:15: Jesus said, "If you love me, you will keep my commandments." Of course we see repeatedly in Scripture that loving God and obeying Him go together (e.g., Exodus 20:6; Deuteronomy 5:10; 7:9; 11:1). But does John 14:15 really mean: "If you act a certain way, you will act a certain way?" If love is only action, then that's what the verse means.

IN 1 CORINTHIANS 13 Paul draws a distinction between action and love. Love, therefore, must be a motivator, an attitude, or an emotion.

---

1 Corinthians 13:1–3: "If I speak in the tongues of men and of angels, but have not love, I am a noisy gong or a clanging cymbal. And if I have prophetic powers, and understand all mysteries and all knowledge, and if I have all faith, so as to remove mountains, but have not love, I am nothing. If I give away all I have, and if I deliver up my body to be burned, but have not love, I gain nothing." Paul implicitly draws a distinction between action— even extraordinarily sacrificial action—and love. Love, therefore, must be a motivator, an attitude, or an emotion.

Romans 5:7–8: "For one will scarcely die for a righteous person—though perhaps for a good person one would dare even to die—but God shows his love for us in that while we were still sinners, Christ died for us." The death of Christ *shows* what would otherwise be hidden: that is, how God feels toward us.

LOVE: A DISPOSITION AND AN EVENT

In chapter 3 we contrasted briefly long-term and short-term joy. To review, with long-term joy we have a person who says to herself, "Life is good." Thus her disposition is toward joy; joy is the typical or characteristic experience of her days. It has emotional content, but it is more subdued. With short-term joy, we have a person who says, "This event is good." That is, because she interprets a particular thing as beneficial, helpful, or leading to peace and security, her reaction is joyful. The emotion is more pronounced. But once the effects of the event are over, joy subsides or disappears.

We can say something very similar about love. We can have a loving disposition. We might recognize this in ourselves as more of an attitude or as more cognitive than emotional. On the other hand, we can have a distinctly emotional loving reaction to a particular event. We could illustrate it this way: suppose a husband is very busy at work, intensely focused on trying to get some concrete poured on time. If you interrupt him and ask, "Do you love your wife?" he could answer truthfully and say "Yes" and go right back to work (it's a guy thing). This love is a disposition.

On the other hand, if during this interruption you report, "Your wife's in the hospital; she was just in a car accident," he will be deeply moved, leave work, and sit by her side at the hospital. This love is more emotional. He does more than register it as a fact; his feelings move him to take action—action not because he's commanded to or expected to, but action because he wants to.

JESUS: MOVED BY HIS DISPOSITION
AND HIS IMMEDIATE FEELINGS OF LOVE

We can illustrate further from the life of Jesus. We would rightly say that He is loving all the time (dispositional). But this love can be seen in particular emotional events. Here are a couple of examples:

Moved by a leper. While Jesus was going through Galilee, preaching and casting out demons, "a leper came to him, imploring him, and kneeling said to him, 'If you will, you can make me clean.' Moved with pity, he stretched out his hand and touched him and said to him, 'I will; be clean'" (Mark 1:39–41). The translation of the ESV, "moved with pity," is good; it might also be translated "felt compassion" (Matthew 14:14, 18:27; Luke 7:13). This word appears repeatedly in the Gospels and always has Jesus as its subject. The particular verb used is an emotional one (*splangchnizomai*). It is related to the word for "insides" or "intestines" (*splangchna*, Acts 1:18) because to feel pity or compassion is to be aware that along with the emotion are changes in our body. We feel it in our gut.

So when Jesus encountered the leper he was visibly moved. But it is not the case that before meeting the man Jesus was loveless. Rather, we see a loving disposition manifested in a particularly loving event.

Moved by one seeking eternal life. Once "a man ran up and knelt before" Jesus, asking:

"Good Teacher, what must I do to inherit eternal life?" And Jesus said to him, "Why do you call me good? No one is good except God alone. You know the commandments: 'Do not murder, Do not commit adultery, Do not steal, Do not bear false witness, Do not defraud, Honor

your father and mother.'" And he said to him, "Teacher,
all these I have kept from my youth." And Jesus, looking
at him, loved him, and said to him, "You lack one thing:
go, sell all that you have and give to the poor, and you will
have treasure in heaven; and come, follow me." (Mark
10:17–21)

What is going on in this encounter? Unlike some other interactions Jesus had with people asking Him questions, there is no
desire to put Jesus to the test (contrast Matthew 22:18 and Luke
10:25). This was an honest question. As author Stephen Vorwinde
writes, "Jesus took a good hard look at the man. He studied him,
and as he did so he was moved with affection for him. There was
something in this young man that was deeply appealing to Jesus.
His answer had not been hypocritical or arrogant."[3]

JESUS' WHOLE LIFE was one of love, from incarnation, to temptation, to preaching, to feeding the crowds, to blessing children.

Only here in Mark is it said that Jesus loved someone. But
surely His whole life was one of love, from incarnation (John
1:14), to temptation (Matthew 4), to preaching (Mark 1:39), to
feeding the crowds (Luke 9:12–16), to blessing children (Mark
10:16). All these acts come from a heart of love. So what do we
make of this love? When Jesus encountered the young man, He
experienced a particular pronounced and visible feeling of love.

How would the man respond? He could not leave the young man in his condition, for there was something he still lacked, something that the Law of Moses also demanded: generosity to the poor (10:21). He called the young man to a literally costly discipleship. Sadly, the man did not respond.

RIGHT AND WRONG KINDS OF LOVES

Scripture gives us several examples to reach the conclusion that love is an emotion having to do with the perceived worth of something. What you perceive to be worthy or valuable, you will seek to acquire, or to protect, or to enjoy.

But just as Scripture speaks of appropriate and inappropriate joys (Psalm 31:7; 1 Corinthians 13:7), and of appropriate and inappropriate kinds of anger (Nehemiah 5:6; Ephesians 4:26), so also it speaks of appropriate (Spirit led) loves and inappropriate (sinful) loves. Let's look first at wrong, or inappropriate, kinds of love.

INAPPROPRIATE LOVES

In terms of inappropriate love, we can begin with physical love. The Scriptures point out that *in the sexual expression of love, selfish lust has no place.* In Genesis 34:2–3 we have a horrid example of sexual assault. After Shechem the Hivite saw Dinah, "he seized her and lay with her and humiliated her. And his soul was drawn to Dinah the daughter of Jacob. He loved the young woman and spoke tenderly to her." For a man to love a woman is a glorious thing, if that love is godly. Shechem loved Dinah, but in this case his love was brutal, self-centered, and motivated by a desire to possess.

A second inappropriate love is a marriage between a believer and nonbeliever. The Old Testament law warned God's people against marrying Gentile spouses, just as the New Testament warns Christ followers not to be unevenly yoked with nonbelievers. Yet we learn "King Solomon loved many foreign women, along with the daughter of Pharaoh: Moabite, Ammonite, Edomite, Sidonian, and Hittite women, from the nations concerning which the Lord had said to the people of Israel, 'You shall not enter into marriage with them, neither shall they with you, for surely they will turn away your heart after their gods.' Solomon clung to these in love" (1 Kings 11:1–2).

Perhaps Solomon's love was driven by a selfish desire for variety, or by a desire to have a political alliance with all these other countries. In any case, it certainly led him to disobey the law of Deuteronomy 17:14–18. The result was these women lured him from a wholehearted worship of God. A key motive in any marriage should be to honor God, whereas marriage between a believer and nonbeliever will tempt the believer to compromise his or her faith.

A third inappropriate love is to love the values of the society, the culture that surrounds us. Here the aged and jailed Paul encourages Timothy to come to him quickly. He says the reason is "Demas, in love with this present world, has deserted me and gone to Thessalonica. Crescens has gone to Galatia, Titus to Dalmatia" (2 Timothy 4:10). Paul is alone. He says nothing of the motivations that Crescens and Titus had for leaving, but the cause of Demas's departure is clear: he loves and lives for "this present world." If Demas had loved Paul, the gospel, and the church, he would not have deserted Paul.

Of course, *another wrong love we all are tempted by is the love of ourselves*. John writes to the church in 3 John 9: "I have written something to the church, but Diotrephes, who loves to be first, does not recognize us" (author translation). Recognizing the apostle John's authority would put Diotrephes second (or worse!). When you or I am first, people look up to us, give us honor, praise us. The idol known as Self enjoys such recognition. So did Diotrephes.

APPROPRIATE LOVES

Our love for God is altogether appropriate, and it should always be primary. Love for a pet or a favorite coffee cup can be genuine and good. But our love for all such lessor objects will be mild and weak compared to our love for God. He has such immense worth and beauty that nothing but a strong love from our whole self will do. Thus He commands, "You shall love the Lord your God with all your heart and with all your soul and with all your might" (Deuteronomy 6:5). What will this love look like? How will it manifest itself? One way is found in the next example—and the next appropriate love we should feel and demonstrate.

Because God Himself is so valuable, then what He says to us is also valuable. Thus the psalmist says, "I will lift up my hands toward your commandments, which I love, and I will meditate on your statutes" (119:48). As Jesus said, if we love God and love His commandments, we will follow those commandments. This is a second appropriate love.

This obedience will be reflected in the way we love people. In contrast to the brutal love displayed by Shechem (Genesis 34:2–3), we find Jacob's love for Rachel. Jacob desired to have Rachel as his wife and so said to her father Laban, "I will serve you seven years for your younger daughter Rachel" (Genesis 29:18).

Such love demonstrates patience and respect. This is the sacrificial love that characterizes marriage. Undoubtedly the most precious example of loving a spouse comes from Ephesians, where Paul calls on men to love their wives to the extent Christ continues to love His church. "Husbands, love your wives, as Christ loved the church and gave himself up for her, that he might sanctify her, having cleansed her by the washing of water with the word, so that he might present the church to himself in splendor" (Ephesians 5:25–27). We see at least that this love is willing to endure pain and seeks the good of the other person.

And of course, we will not only love our spouse. We will love parents, children, and also God's people, as this next example shows: "Therefore, my brothers, whom I love and long for, my joy and crown, stand firm thus in the Lord, my beloved" (Philippians 4:1). Paul loved all the churches he planted, but the Philippians were special. Unlike any other, they were partners with him in the advance of the gospel.

THE SUM OF OUR FEELINGS

From TV, movies, magazines, and blogs we typically get an inferior understanding of love. It is weak, fickle, and has to do only with emotion. On the other hand, to correct such a poor view of love, some well-meaning believers have swung the pendulum too far in the other direction. They say love is only action. But such a definition is also inferior, indeed, even pharisaic.

Love and action go together, but love is a motivator for action. It is moved by the value it sees in a person or thing, takes pleasure or delight in the person or thing—such as a good meal, the Lord Jesus, or a neighbor—and then acts appropriately: it partakes with thanksgiving and sharing, it worships and serves, it seeks the good (respectively).

Just as there are appropriate and inappropriate joys, appropriate and inappropriate kinds of anger, so also there are appropriate loves and inappropriate loves. Although exceptions exist, most often in Scripture the appropriateness of our love has to do with the object of our love. Love for God is good; love for the world is not. Love for brothers and sisters in Christ is good; love for the best seat in church is not. Love for the advance of the gospel is good; love for more money is not.

We can think of most emotions two ways: as a disposition or as an event. So we know of people who are easily irritated (having a disposition toward anger) and we know of particular times when they really blow their cool (an angry event). So also with love; we can have a tendency to value people (loving disposition), and we can feel special compassion for an individual in need (loving event). We should seek to cultivate both of these loves.

Toward a Healthy Emotional Life

If love has such a deeply internal and emotional element, and if godly love is *both* affection (emotional content) *and* action, how do we cultivate such love? We need to remember, as we said in chapter 2, that emotions grow out of convictions or beliefs. The more our convictions are in conformity with all of Scripture, the more we expect our love to be godly. Here are some steps:

1. *Receive the love of God so you can pass love on to others.* Before we can love, we must be loved. But even the love of the godliest mother and father will not fully prepare us to love. We need to receive the love of God in Christ. The apostle John says straightforwardly, "We love because he first loved us" (1 John 4:19).

   In some ways this love of God is unlike human love. Paul says, "Christ died for the ungodly. For one will scarcely die for a righteous person—though perhaps for a good person one would dare even to die—but God shows his love for us in that while we were still sinners, Christ died for us" (Romans 5:6–8). Humans typically love the worthy, the good, and the righteous. God loved us, His enemies, and transformed us into His children. In order to understand it better, ponder such passages as Matthew 26:59–27:46; John 19:1–36; and Philippians 2:5–11.

2. *Make love a concern of prayer.* If we want a godly love, it will not come merely by human effort. We must cast ourselves on the mercy of God for such a love to take root in us. Pray daily a prayer such as Philippians 1:9–11 and Ephesians 3:14–19, which ends, "Be strengthened with power through his Spirit in your inner being, so that Christ may dwell in your hearts

through faith—that you, being rooted and grounded in love, may have strength . . . to know the love of Christ that surpasses knowledge, that you may be filled with all the fullness of God" (Ephesians 3:16–19).

As you pray, personalize your words. You might say, "God, I know that my love is often foolish. Please make my love grow in knowledge and discernment."

3. *Develop your love by imitating God and Christ.* God puts surprising value on people. Even though we are weak, He grants us great honor (Psalm 8). So to imitate God is to walk in love and value other people as God values us (Ephesians 5:1–2). A few times in Scripture we find specific calls to pattern our thinking, compassion, and action after Christ. For example, read and meditate on 1 Corinthians 10:32–11:1 and 1 Peter 2:21–23. A classic passage to help with a Christlike pattern of thinking is Philippians 2:5–8:

Have this mind among yourselves, which is yours in Christ Jesus, who, though he was in the form of God, did not count equality with God a thing to be grasped, but emptied himself, taking the form of a servant, being born in the likeness of men. And being found in human form, he humbled himself by becoming obedient to the point of death, even death on a cross.

4. *Develop your skills in showing love by knowing others better.* Sometimes we might mistakenly assume that if we have the best intentions, then our love will be of the highest quality. But godly love is richer than that. Thus Peter commands husbands to "live with your wives in an understanding way, showing honor to the woman as the weaker vessel, since they are heirs with you of the grace of life, so that your prayers may

not be hindered" (1 Peter 3:7). The phrase "in an understanding way" is literally "according to knowledge" and implies that becoming a student of your wife will improve your love for her. Similarly Paul prays for Philippian believers that their "love may abound more and more, with knowledge and all discernment" (Philippians 1:9).

The Thessalonian believers had "been taught by God to love one another," and they demonstrated that love "to all the brothers throughout Macedonia" (1 Thessalonians 4:9–10). This teaching from God might come directly from the guidance of His Holy Spirit on our lives and actions. On the other hand, this teaching may come from older and wiser Christians (for example, see Titus 2:3–5).

5. *Listen to the constructive criticism of others.* Those who are close to us know us well. They can see our motivations day after day. Many times my dear wife has pointed out my inferior, selfish, and otherwise unloving motivations. This is painful, yet it is valuable to hear. Give a close friend or your spouse the right to tell you if he/she thinks your motivations are less than they should be. Ask them how you can love better and listen carefully to the response.

Questions for Discussion

1. Has it been or is it now your opinion that "Love is not an emotion, it's an action"? Explain where your opinion came from.
2. Discuss: "We typically do not want action without proper emotion."
3. Read and discuss the connection between love and action seen in Exodus 20:6; Deuteronomy 5:10, 7:9, 11:1.
4. React to this definition of love: "Love is an emotion that has

to do with the perceived worth of something; we put a positive emotion onto what we consider valuable." How would you
improve the definition?
5. Would you say that you have experienced God's love both intellectually and emotionally? If so, share examples. If not, tell
why.
6. Reread 1 Thessalonians 4:9–11 and Titus 2:3–5. What skills do
you need in order to love in a godly and wise way?

Suggestions for Further Reading

Chapman, Gary. *The 5 Love Languages: The Secret to Love That
Lasts.* Chicago: Northfield, 2010.
Eggerichs, Emerson. *Love and Respect.* Nashville: Nelson, 2004.

8 ◆ *Fear:* A Good Kind and a Bad Kind

I AM A REAL WIMP when it comes to amusement park rides. Even the little spinning teacups of the Mad Tea Party at Disney World put me on the edge. Forget roller coasters. Some people will shout for joy when they are flying down at 50 miles per hour. Not me. I can't catch my breath from fear. Raise my hands? No way. I am clinching the bar or seat belt with white knuckles.

Once I went with the family to Six Flags over Texas. We went on this drop ride, an older version of their current Superman Tower of Power. You go straight up thirty-two stories and then you drop; it is pure terror. We were only a few feet off the ground when I felt my first regret. Of course, it was too late. Up and up and up we went. There should be a law against being up so high when you are not in an airplane.

And then, for what seemed like an eternity, we stopped, suspended more than three hundred feet above the ground. Then the worst happened. We dropped.

I could not breathe. My whole body went tense. Afterward, I walked the park with horrible back pain—for the rest of the day. I look back on that wild day in Arlington, Texas, and wonder why we had to pay for such torture.

You could call my fear unreasonable and that would be fine with me. You might say, "Statistically, more people get killed in auto accidents than in amusement park accidents. So your fear is unreasonable." I admit it is unreasonable, but it is a real fear nevertheless.

Some unreasonable fears are not helpful for us. But we have

to admit that sometimes fear is good. Without fear many of us would be dead. We fear pain, and such fear has often kept us wearing our safety belt, away from knives or thin ice, and on a healthy diet. But fear has also kept us from financial giving, from evangelism, from volunteering at church, from confronting a brother or sister who needs correction, and from all sorts of obedience to God.

WHAT DO YOU FEAR?

What is fear? To help define it, we should keep in mind that fear always has at least two parts. First, there is the thing that we are *fearful of*. This might be something concrete or definite like the dentist's office, an exam, the yearly performance review at work, public speaking, or walking home late at night. It might be something abstract like infertility, unemployment, being a failure at life, loneliness, or rejection. In all cases we have a thing or a situation that provokes fear.

But second, there is the thing that we are *fearful about*. The dentist's office might bring physical pain, while the exam could bring a sense of failure. Walking home late makes us vulnerable to crime. The prospects of being infertile, unemployed (or in the wrong line of work), and lonely all present to us a life that is unfulfilled. Valued goals are not met, and we are left empty, frustrated, discouraged. That is, what we fear is always future and always interpreted as harmful/painful.

In all these cases fear involves a negative emotion in the present—call it dread, or anxiety, or worry. But all these emotional reactions have to do with our anticipation of a future event (for example, being lonely without children, being robbed and beaten, living in poverty). We expect that this future event will cause us pain: either literal physical pain or more emotional pain.

This looking forward brings a negative feeling in the present. That present emotion is a type of fear. We might call it anxiety or worry or dread. All of these are in the same category. We fear a doctor's report. *Will she say it is cancer?* We fear an interview. *Am I going to get this job? I really need it!* We fear an exam. *I don't want my classmates to think I'm stupid!*

Fears vary from person to person. You might think roller coasters are great; I think they are ridiculous. Our own unique approach to fear will depend on a lot of things:

* *Our family.* Parents might have passed on to us helpful and true or false and destructive fears. Some parents instill fear not by what they teach but by how they behave and how they treat children and each other.
* *Our personality and thinking.* Every parent knows that their children have different personalities. Depending on our personality, we can think our way into false or correct fears.
* *Trauma we have suffered.* Events can leave deep long-term fear. Physical debilitation may result from trauma or illness, and along with it, fearful thoughts.
* *Our economic or social status.* The poor might fear oppression and hardship; the rich might fear crime and the indignation of the poor.
* *Our view of God.* Even if we have been Christians since childhood, we can still have distorted views of God.

FEAR: IS IT GOOD OR IS IT BAD?

Can fear ever be good? Indeed it can. In his book *Feelings and Faith: Cultivating Godly Emotions in the Christian Life,* Pastor Brian S. Borgman rightly says that there is a good kind of fear "that helps preserve our lives."[1] Without fear, we would subject ourselves to dangers and fatal situations. For example, I regularly walk in downtown Chicago between Union Station and the office. Mostly this is pleasant; it's a good way to get a little exercise at the beginning and end of the workday. But taxis are something to watch out for. On the one hand, I sympathize with taxi drivers: they don't get paid by the hour; it's not productive to sit around waiting for a pedestrian. And I certainly would not enjoy driving all day long. On the other hand, they always seem to take unnecessary risks and drive too fast; several times a taxi has come within a few inches of me.

So as a pedestrian in downtown Chicago I need to exercise healthy fear. You might call it caution. I imagine that ending up beneath the tires of a cab would be painful (a thought about the possible future). So in the present I have a small amount of fear.

Fear recognizes that the environment we live in is sometimes dangerous. We all live with these kinds of dangers:

- The weather forecaster projects twenty inches of heavy snow, or a line of thunderstorms with hail.
- Your family has a history of schizophrenia and you start to show symptoms.
- The teacher calls you up to speak in front of the class.
- The factory has announced that there will be cutbacks in the number of employees at all levels in the company.
- You get a call from the police saying that your teenage son was injured in the cross-fire of gang violence.

All these situations can invoke fear. In all cases fear should cause us to take all the appropriate action we can, such as preparing for the storm, seeing a doctor, taking a deep breath and facing your classmates, looking for another job, or rushing to the hospital. Such fear that leads to appropriate action is good.

Even though Borgman recognizes that fear can be good, later in his book he adds,

> The Bible leaves no room for debate. The source of fear, worry, and anxiety is unbelief. The unbelief is specific, spelled out to us by Isaiah and Jesus. When we fail to believe that God is for us, will take care of us, has our future in his hands, and is with us right now, we cave in to fear, worry, or anxiety.[2]

Is all fear really a lack of faith? Let's suppose that this view is correct: all fear has to do with failure to trust God. Imagine this: There's a guy you know who is all stressed about some important events coming up in his life. You can tell that he's anxious . . . very anxious. He even says that he's really troubled. He seems tense, his forehead glistens with perspiration.

You say to him, "Hey, doesn't Psalm 34:4 say, 'I sought the Lord, and he answered me and delivered me from all my fears'? Have you prayed about this? Doesn't Matthew 6:25 say, 'Therefore I tell you, do not be anxious about your life'? And didn't Paul say in Philippians 4:6, 'Do not be anxious about anything, but in everything by prayer and supplication with thanksgiving let your requests be made known to God'? Maybe all your anxiety is from a lack of faith. You're obviously afraid. I think fear at times is just the opposite of faith. And we all know that the Bible says, 'Do not fear.'

"Besides, all things work together for the good. So I'm sure that you should be looking forward to the happy ending God will bring out of this."

I can imagine what the response could be. Now I use the

word "could" in a loose sense. But imagine what the response could be. The person you have reprimanded for fear and anxiety might turn to you and say, "Peter, I told you to wait over there while I go pray. Go back to James and John!"

KING JESUS IN THE GARDEN: A CASE STUDY

And now, consider Jesus in Gethsemane. Did Jesus have fear while in the garden of Gethsemane? If so, was such fear good? The events of Gethsemane let us know that *there are times when fear is good, even virtuous.* Let's take a deeper look.

Before the garden. In the days leading up to His betrayal at Gethsemane, Jesus had already predicted that in Jerusalem He would be rejected, mocked, abused, and executed by crucifixion. In these predictions He also said He would be resurrected (Matthew 16:21, 17:23, 20:19; Mark 14:28; Luke 9:22, 18:33). So at one level, Jesus was not surprised by anything that would happen in Gethsemane that night.

In the garden. What makes the garden of Gethsemane significant? Jesus knew there would be no going back after this. Judas has already abandoned the group of disciples so that he can lead the high priest's crowd to Jesus. The betrayer has been with Jesus and the other disciples in the garden many times; Judas knows where to look for them. Jesus waits, anticipating the arrest, the abandonment, the brutality.

MATTHEW AND MARK ON THE FEAR OF JESUS

The three gospels that tell of these events in the garden tell us slightly different things (complementary things, not contradictory things). So sweat "like blood" and angelic aid are unique to Luke (22:43–44).[3] We'll discuss those verses later. In both Matthew and Mark we find Jesus in great distress. They read,

> And taking with him Peter and the two sons of Zebedee, he began to be sorrowful and troubled. Then he said to them, "My soul is very sorrowful, even to death; remain here, and watch with me." And going a little farther he fell on his face and prayed, saying, "My Father, if it be possible, let this cup pass from me; nevertheless, not as I will, but as you will." (Matthew 26:37–39)

> And he took with him Peter and James and John, and began to be greatly distressed and troubled. And he said to them, "My soul is very sorrowful, even to death. Remain here and watch." And going a little farther, he fell on the ground and prayed that, if it were possible, the hour might pass from him. (Mark 14:33–35)

Both Matthew and Mark use strong language. Being "grieved" or "sorrowful" is common in the gospels (Matthew 14:9, 18:31; Mark 10:22, 14:19; John 16:20). The word for "troubled" has to do with distress or anxiety; the word appears only here and in Philippians 2:26.

The strongest language, however, is the phrase "very sorrowful, even to death" (Matthew 26:38). It describes a deep sadness or grief that is crushing and feels like the very end of life itself (death). The words are reminiscent of Psalm 42:6 and 43:5, except that the psalmist eventually finds relief instead of death; Jesus does not.

LUKE ON THE FEAR OF JESUS

But perhaps you are not convinced that Jesus was afraid. *He was sorrowful, but was He actually feeling fear? Why say that He was?* First, the very prayer Jesus prays tells of fear: "Father, if you are willing, remove this cup from me" (Luke 22:42). The "cup" is an image often used in the Old Testament to speak of the wrath of God. So Jeremiah 25:15–16 says, "Thus the Lord, the God of Israel, said to me: 'Take from my hand this cup of the wine of wrath, and make all the nations to whom I send you drink it. They shall drink and stagger and be crazed because of the sword that I am sending among them.'" Those familiar with the Old Testament know that the wrath of God is nothing to take lightly. His wrath destroyed most of the ancient world except for Noah and his family (Genesis 6–9); His wrath opened a fissure in the earth that "swallowed all the people who belonged to Korah and all their goods" (Numbers 16:32).

Yet those instances of wrath were temporary. The cross of Christ is the ultimate and final solution to wrath. It is this wrath that Jesus begins to see in the garden, and it is terror.

But other things Luke says make it clear that Jesus was afraid. While praying He is in "agony" (Greek *agōnia*), a word that appears in the New Testament only in Luke 22:44, and in this context it refers to emotional turmoil. Surely this emotional turmoil is not the angry frustration that comes from driving in a traffic jam or from trying to figure out a difficult math problem. No, Jesus is in dread of the Cross and the abandonment it will mean for Him.

Further, Luke says that the sweat of Jesus "became like great drops of blood falling down to the ground" (v. 44). Perhaps this is just a simile used to describe how profuse his sweat was. If so, it describes an aspect of the anxiety Jesus was going through. More likely, in my view, it is literal. Bloody sweat is technically known as *hemathidrosis*, a rare but documented medical phenomenon.[4] In hemathidrosis severe anxiety can cause capillaries in the skin to rupture, allowing blood into the sweat glands thus producing bloody sweat.

But why should such dreadful agony come on Jesus now? Because this is the last temptation to take the painless way out of His mission. Satan's temptations of Jesus in the wilderness all offered Him an easy, painless way to prove the care of God and obtain glory. In Luke 4:13 we find that "when the devil had ended every temptation, he departed from him until an opportune time."

JESUS FACES A CHOICE. He can run from the betrayal and so escape the torture of the cross. Or He can obey His Father and endure wrath.

What was that opportune time? The Gospel does not say so explicitly, but I take it that it is the time starting with the betrayal and ending with Jesus' death. Consider the following passages in Luke 22:

> Then Satan entered into Judas called Iscariot, who was of the number of the twelve. He went away and conferred with the chief priests and officers how he might betray

him to them (vv. 3–4). *Satan now acts in a unique way with Judas.*

"Simon, Simon, behold, Satan demanded to have you, that he might sift you like wheat, but I have prayed for you that your faith may not fail. And when you have turned again, strengthen your brothers" (Luke 22:31–32). *Now Satan wants Peter not only to disown Jesus during His time of agony, but to disown Him and never repent.*

Luke 22:52–53: Then Jesus said to the chief priests and officers of the temple and elders, who had come out against him, "Have you come out as against a robber, with swords and clubs? When I was with you day after day in the temple, you did not lay hands on me. But this is your hour, and the power of darkness." *Why would Jesus be arrested now and not months earlier? It is because now is the dark hour—that is, Satan's time.*

Jesus faces a choice, a doorway. He can run from the betrayal and arrest and so escape the torture of the cross. Or He can obey His Father and endure wrath. We need to see that the choice is not easy. He makes the right choice, proves again that He always does His Father's will (John 5:19, 6:38, 8:29), and goes to execution. Nevertheless, there is turmoil. Such turmoil is probably also seen in these words from Hebrews 5:7–8: "In the days of his flesh, Jesus offered up prayers and supplications, with loud cries and tears, to him who was able to save him from death, and he was heard because of his reverence. Although he was a son, he learned obedience through what he suffered."

Let's remind ourselves of a couple of vital truths that we mentioned in chapter 2: Jesus is both sinless and virtuous. First, as sinless He can be the perfect sacrifice for sins. But also we can work with the assumption that any emotion we detect with Jesus is a sinless manifestation of the emotion. If He was afraid, *then there are times when we can experience a sinless fear.* Second, Jesus is virtuous. God the Father said of the Son, "You are my beloved Son; with you I am well pleased" (Luke 3:22). As mentioned above, Jesus always did His Father's will. Thus, Jesus is our example not only of bad things to be avoided (sins) but also of good things to be imitated (virtue).

To say it again, imitating Jesus means imitating both His action and His emotion. Jesus' fear of the cross was godly. Most importantly, we need to see that Jesus obeyed His Father even though the Son was horribly afraid. We will return to fear and obedience later.

OTHER INSTANCES OF GOOD FEAR

In Numbers 12 Aaron and Miriam grew jealous of Moses' power and authority and challenged him. In response the Lord said, "Hear my words: If there is a prophet among you, I the Lord make myself known to him in a vision; I speak with him in a dream. Not so with my servant Moses. He is faithful in all my house. With him I speak mouth to mouth, clearly, and not in riddles, and he beholds the form of the Lord. Why then were you not afraid to speak against my servant Moses?" (vv. 6–8). Those whom God has put in authority over us ought to receive our healthy fear—perhaps better called "respect" (1 Corinthians 16:16; 1 Thessalonians 5:12; Hebrews 13:17). Honoring authorities is a way to please God (1 Thessalonians 4:1), and we ought to fear displeasing God. We fear, not because of a worry about eternal punishment, but because we know that God can be grieved by our disobedience (Ephesians 4:30).

In Romans 13 Paul commands submission to government and says that it "is God's servant for your good. But if you do wrong, be afraid, for he does not bear the sword in vain. For he is the servant of God, an avenger who carries out God's wrath on the wrongdoer" (v. 4). Here we find fear as a motivator for avoiding punishment. Certainly there are better motivations for obedience than fear, but fear is a motivator not to be ignored. (Jesus used fear as a motivator as well; see Luke 12:4–5.)

Further, Paul described the way for Timothy to treat elders, saying, "As for those who persist in sin, rebuke them in the presence of all, so that the rest may stand in fear" (1 Timothy 5:20). We ought to fear sin, and not just because of possible rebuke. Paul exhorts the Corinthians, saying, "Since we have these promises, beloved, let us cleanse ourselves from every defilement of body and spirit, bringing holiness to completion in the fear of God" (2 Corinthians 7:1). Those who purify themselves make themselves more effective in ministry, as Paul exhorted Timothy: "Therefore, if anyone cleanses himself from what is dishonorable, he will be a vessel for honorable use, set apart as holy, useful to the master of the house, ready for every good work" (2 Timothy 2:21). Surely we want to avoid the grief of knowing that sin has made us less effective.

UNGODLY FEAR:
KING SAUL AMONG THE AMALEKITES

But surely not all fear is good. The repeated command of Scripture, "Do not be afraid" has to mean something (for example, Genesis 46:3; Joshua 10:25; Nehemiah 4:14; Proverbs 3:25; Acts 18:9). Let's turn to an example of ungodly fear.

After being in the Promised Land for many years, the people of Israel asked for a king (1 Samuel 8). Their first king was Saul. Fear is a primary element that leads to Saul's disastrous kingship. We have seen that some fears are very good; some not so. Thus, it is not fear in itself, but the wrong kind of fear (fear with the wrong object, fear with a wrong motivation) that leads to Saul's failure. Let's look at a few episodes in his life.

First Episode (1 Samuel 10:17–24). By the command of God, the prophet Samuel anointed Saul as king (10:1). Sometime later there was a public gathering where Saul was shown to indeed be God's choice for king and not just Samuel's choice. The people gathered and cast lots to determine who was God's choice, moving from the large group of the tribe to the smaller and smaller groups of clan and family until finally the lot fell to Saul. But when the people looked for Saul, he was not around. The passage says God Himself revealed Saul's location: "Behold, he has hidden himself among the baggage" (v. 22).

Now the passage does not use the term "fear," but that has to be what it is. Saul's fear may seem very natural. I imagine that kingship over a few million rebellious people is no easy task. And he was the first person to have the role. We might think such fear was natural, but only if we did not know the rest of the story—from this little hint we soon learn that Saul has a problem with fear. More examples will appear throughout his life. Like Adam, Saul is running away from his God-given responsibilities (Genesis 3:8–10).

Second Episode (1 Samuel 13:8–13). In the first test of Saul's kingship, a great number of Philistines assemble for battle against Israel. Saul is supposed to wait for Samuel, who will come and offer the sacrifice (1 Samuel 10:8). The prophet says clearly, "Seven days you shall wait, until I come to you and show you what you shall do." But when it appears that Samuel is late, Saul becomes impatient and gives the burnt offering himself because "the people were scattering from him" (13:8; cf. vv. 11–12).

What would motivate this? Is there any scriptural prece-
dent or teaching that says a large number of soldiers is needed
to win a battle? No, not at all! Saul forgot all about what God
did with Gideon. Back in Judges God trimmed down Gideon's
army from thirty-two thousand to three hundred (Judges 7:1–7).
But Gideon's army still won the battle! Jonathan, Saul's son, said
it well in 1 Samuel in 14:6: "Nothing can hinder the Lord from
saving by many or by few." But caught in the fear that the people might abandon the battle and their faith in him as king, Saul
makes his own decision, refusing to heed the call of God through
the prophet Samuel. Unlike the godly fear of Jesus, Saul's fear
leads him to disobey God.

RATHER THAN FEARING God and having a
great concern for the Lord's command, Saul
feared the people and had a great concern
for their request.

Third Episode (1 Samuel 15:1–24). Saul has another chance
to prove his obedience to God. Samuel commands Saul, "Now go
and strike Amalek and devote to destruction all that they have"
(v. 3). But Saul did not devote all to destruction; he saved Agag
the king of Amalek and the best of the livestock. He said he did
this because he feared the soldiers and obeyed their voice (v. 24).
Rightly does Proverbs 29:25 say, "The fear of man lays a snare,

but whoever trusts in the Lord is safe." Rather than fearing God and having a great concern for the Lord's command (listening to His voice), Saul feared the people and had a great concern for their request (listening to their voice). Why? What's the wrong object or the wrong motivation? He wants the honor of people more than the honor of God. We see this in verse 30. Even after he admitted that he sinned, he begs for Samuel to go with him so that he will be honored before the people. Unlike the fear of Jesus, Saul's fear leads him to disobey God.

Fourth Episode (1 Samuel 18:11–29). Saul is jealous of David and tries twice in one day to kill him (v. 11); he fails both times. From this Saul concludes that the Lord is with David. The Scripture says, "Saul was afraid of David because the Lord was with him but had departed from Saul" (v. 12). This is very ironic, isn't it? When Saul tries to kill David, it is Saul who is afraid, not David! "And when Saul saw that [David] had great success, he stood in fearful awe of him" (v. 15).

Later Saul finds out that his daughter Michal loves David (v. 20). So Saul gives her in marriage to David thinking that "she may be a snare for him and that the hand of the Philistines may be against him." The plan is to require that David kill one hundred Philistines as the cost of having Michal as a wife. With this plan Saul hopes to kill David indirectly. But David is successful. What happens then? Saul sees that David is so successful and is not happy but afraid—even more afraid than before (vv. 28–29).

Saul's fear, unlike Jesus' fear, leads to jealousy, disobedience, and anger.

THE SUM OF OUR FEELINGS

Fear can be good. Without fear we would endanger ourselves daily, for the world can be a deadly place at times. Healthy fears give us respect for our boss, cause us to drive more slowly when it's storming, and keep us away from downed power lines.

In keeping with the cognitive theory of emotion (see chapter 2), fears can vary significantly from person to person. Our own unique approach to fear will depend on a lot of things: our upbringing, our personality and thinking, trauma we have suffered, our social location, and our view of God.

Some Christians view fear as the opposite of faith. But I think it's not that simple. We have good reason to believe that the turmoil Jesus experienced in the garden of Gethsemane was a kind of fear. Both Matthew and Mark report that Jesus began to be greatly distressed and troubled (Matthew 26:37–39; Mark 14:33–35). The word for "troubled" has to do with distress or anxiety. According to Mark, Jesus said, "My soul is very sorrowful, even to death" (14:34). These comments demonstrate that Jesus felt dread at the prospect of undergoing divine wrath on the cross. But since Jesus is sinless, His fear was not wrong; it was virtuous.

Still, not all fear is good. A key factor is obedience. Will our fear keep us from it? In the case of Jesus, it did not. In the case of King Saul, his fears repeatedly caused disobedience, for he had the wrong object to his fear. Whereas he should have feared God, he feared man. Many times when the Scripture says, "Do not be afraid," one clear implication is that fear can lead to rejecting God's Word, turning away from God, and disobeying His commands.

Toward a Healthy Emotional Life

1. *Feel free to name your fears to others and to God.* Jesus mentioned His anxiety to the disciples, saying, "My soul is very sorrowful, even to death; remain here, and watch with me"

(Matthew 26:38). Believers in both testaments feel free to name their fears to God. Before his three friends Job confesses his fear: "The thing that I fear comes upon me, and what I dread befalls me. I am not at ease, nor am I quiet; I have no rest, but trouble comes" (Job 3:25–26). King David feared being abandoned by God and the loss of his friend (Psalm 88:14–18); he stated his fear to God directly in song and psalm but also recognized the antidote to such fear: "When I am afraid, I put my trust in you" (Psalm 56:3). And when Ananias heard God's call to aid the newly converted Saul, he confesses his fear before God: "Lord, I have heard from many about this man, how much evil he has done to your saints at Jerusalem. And here he has authority from the chief priests to bind all who call on your name" (Acts 9:13–14).

2. *Ask yourself questions about the source of your fears.* Just as God asked Cain and Jonah about their anger (Genesis 4:1–7; Jonah 4:1–9; see chapter 5), so also it is good to ask ourselves the question that Jesus brought to the Twelve. They were terrified when caught in a storm on the Sea of Galilee. Jesus stilled the storm and said to the disciples, "Why are you so afraid? Have you still no faith?" (Mark 4:40). The Lord's term (*deilos*) is harsh, sometimes associated with a cowardly unreasonable fear (Revelation 21:8; Judges 9:4; 2 Chronicles 13:7). Our fears might be selfish like the fear of the Pharisees (Matthew 21:25–27). Our fears might be foolish. But prayer, reflection, the guidance of the Holy Spirit, pondering Scripture, and the counsel of godly brothers and sisters can help us discern what our fears are about.

3. *Expect crises and expect fear.* It might sound like a contradiction, but crisis is normal. Crises come to us as a regular part

of living. Since crisis is normal, fear is normal. Not to have these is to be more spiritual than Jesus. Remember, Romans 8:28 does teach the certainty that God will bring good out of all our trials and pain. But the certainty of coming through or having victory over our fears does not take them away. Jesus was sure of His future and Jesus was afraid.

Thus we should expect that we will face unique times of stress, pain, anxiety, fear, or discouragement. On the other hand, if we are on an emotional roller coaster every day, we need to get help—a counselor, a doctor, a spiritual advisor, perhaps all three. There is no shame in seeking help when we need it. Emotional stability is not wrong—unless it's emotional denial.

4. *Accept the fears of others even as you encourage them in the faith.* Treat your fearful brothers and sisters the way you want to be treated when you are afraid. Many times the fears of others make us very uncomfortable, so much so that we do not love them—that's too risky. Instead we advise them or correct them. It might be that if we are asking people to be without anxiety, we are asking them to refuse to see the seriousness of their situation. It might be that if we ask people to be without anxiety all the time we are asking them to be shallow people, not to be as open and honest as Jesus—who told His three closest disciples, "I am sorrowful, so pray." If we ask people to be without anxiety all the time we may not be asking them to do something Christlike, but rather something pagan—to follow a Stoic philosopher like Epictetus rather than the example of Jesus.

5. *Pray about your fear.* Fear cannot be shut off. Fear can, however, be minimized if we no longer see the future as threat-

ening. One way to see a better future is prayer. In prayer we bring all our requests, longings, desires, and goals to God. We could paraphrase Philippians 4:6 this way: "If you are anxious about something, that's a good indication it is the very thing you ought to pray most about." If anxiety regularly leads to prayer, then in a sense anxiety does not hinder our relationship with God; it helps it.

6. *Let your fear lead to action.* Fear need not be an end in itself. Fears can lead to action. Paul's fear about the Corinthians leads him to send a letter teaching, rebuking, encouraging, and pleading. Throughout the Bible, however, we find God calling us to obedience based on fear of Him (for example, Leviticus 19:14; Deuteronomy 6:2; 2 Corinthians 5:11; Ephesians 5:21).

7. *Cultivate a godly fear.* As we indicated, there is a good fear, and we can develop it. While it is not our goal to live in terror of God, it is good to have a healthy reverence and respect based on His holiness, power, and right to discipline. Ponder those verses of Scripture that make these truths clear, such as Isaiah 6:1–10. Remember that the goal of godly fear is worship and obedience.

Another way to cultivate godly fear is to cultivate biblical contentment and a holy longing for the glorious future God has for us. We turn to these in our next chapter.

Questions for Discussion

1. Reflect on this definition from early in this chapter: "Fear is a negative emotion in the present—call it dread, or anxiety, or

worry—that has to do with perceived future pain" (either literal physical pain or emotional pain).

2. Evaluate this statement: "All fear has to do with failure to trust God."

3. The author says, "Jesus was sure of His future and Jesus was afraid." In your own words explain how it is that both certainty and fear can exist at the same time. As a help, reread Matthew 16:21, 17:23, 20:19, and 26:37–39.

4. How do you typically react when a Christian expresses fear? Explain why you react that way.

5. Have you ever asked questions about your fears? If not, why not? If so, what answers have you come up with?

Suggestions for Further Reading

Allender, Dan and Tremper Longman III. *The Cry of the Soul: How Our Emotions Reveal Our Deepest Questions about God.* Colorado Springs: NavPress, 1994.

Smith, Rhett. *The Anxious Christian: Can God Use Your Anxiety for Good?* Chicago: Moody, 2011.

9 ♦ *Contentment* and *Holy Longing*

MOST CHRISTIANS ARE familiar with the virtue called contentment. They understand that contentment has an emotional aspect to it and would rightly define it as "feeling okay" about something or "being at peace" with something. The most important passage in Scripture dealing with contentment is Philippians 4. Even though the apostle Paul is under arrest in Rome, he says, "I have learned in whatever situation I am to be content" (v. 11b). Very often this contentment, and how we should apply it to ourselves, is described this way:

What did [Paul] learn? What was he taught? What did he know? And who taught him? Paul learned to be *autarkê*, which means self-sufficient or content. Contentment—this is what the Lord taught him in prison. He learned to be self-sufficient, independent of all the changing circumstances of life. He learned to be able to live independent of everything, but dependent on God and God alone. . . .

Paul learned he could have deep peace in his soul, whatever his circumstances. He learned he could pray instead of murmuring and sing instead of sulking. Thus, when he was led to preach in Europe in the city of Philippi, and this Roman citizen, this accomplished rabbi and apostle of Christ, was stripped and severely beaten and thrown into an inner cell in the Philippian jail where his feet were placed in stocks, he, together with Silas, began to pray and sing hymns at midnight. This is true contentment, true happiness that is irrespective of circumstances. . . .

Paul was taught by the Lord to be content, to be happy and rejoice in all situations.[1]

There is much that is helpful in this description. True contentment has to do with our trust in God. It is not something that comes to us naturally; we need to learn it. We can have contentment even in the midst of disappointment and pain. We will talk more about these elements later.

AT ONE AND THE SAME time we have cause for peace and cause for lack of peace; reason for calm and reason for restlessness.

But there is much in the above description of Paul and contentment that is not helpful. The issue is what "all situations" means. I have often heard believers say that Paul means absolutely any possible type of situation. Is that right? Does it mean that when the poor are oppressed, we should "be at peace"? The prophet Amos wasn't! He preached an impassioned rebuke and call to repentance (Amos 4:1–3). Does it mean that when people are hard-hearted and unrepentant we should "feel okay" with that? Jesus wasn't! In the next chapter we will see how Christ wept over Jerusalem because of the people's stubborn ignorance (Luke 19:37–44). Does it mean that when people are taught false doctrine and led away into sin, we should "rejoice in that situation"? Paul didn't! In such situations he was rightly angry (2 Corinthians 11:29).

Why is it important to clarify that contentment does not

apply to absolutely everything? The clarification is important because we are in an inaugurated kingdom, a now-and-not-yet existence. Jesus is Lord of all heaven and earth, but His lordship is contested. While He is working to accomplish His will, the Devil, his angels, and unbelievers live in rebellion. Thus, at one and the same time we have cause for peace and cause for lack of peace, grounds for joy and for groaning, reason for calm and reason for restlessness. So in this chapter I will be asserting two things:

1. If we feel nothing in our life but anxiety, discouragement, anger, and the like, then we do not understand the glory and blessing of what has been given us in the gospel. That is, we do not see the "already." The "already" leads to contentment.
2. If we feel nothing in our life but peace and joy, then we cannot or will not see the pain and suffering around us, pain that ought to move us as well. Plus, we might just be in denial about our own pain. That is, we do not see the "not yet." That will lead us to legitimate groaning.

WHAT IS CONTENTMENT?

To understand the nature of true contentment, we must start with Philippians 4. Paul responds to a gift the Philippian church sent him while he was under arrest in Rome. On the one hand, the gift brings him great joy (v. 10); it is sharing with him in his pain (v. 14). The gift reflects maturity and love on the part of the Philippians (vv. 10, 15–16).

On the other hand, even though Paul considers the gift a good thing, he states that he does not seek economic support (v. 17). The reason is his contentment. He describes the contentment this way:

Not that I am speaking of being in need, for I have
learned in whatever situation I am to be content. I know
how to be brought low, and I know how to abound. In
any and every circumstance, I have learned the secret of
facing plenty and hunger, abundance and need. I can do
all things through him who strengthens me. (Philippians
4:11–13).

The phrase "do all things" in verse 13 should be understood
in the context as "be content in all financial situations." Certainly
by saying "I can do all things," he does not mean that he can do
impossible things such as never sleeping; he does not mean he
can do blasphemous things such as becoming God. He means
he can do the things mentioned in verse 12—he faces life with
contentment, whether he has plenty or little.

So Philippians 4:11–13 teaches that contentment has to do
with our attitude toward, or our emotional response to, financial
situations. Poverty does not lead to anxiety and to greed (Matthew
6:24–26), and wealth does not lead to arrogance and worry of what
I might lose (as it does in Psalm 73:3–6). Rather we are content.

Every other occurrence of "content" and "contentment" in
the New Testament likewise refers to finances.[2]

- In *Luke 3* soldiers come to John the Baptist and ask
  him what fruit they should bear that demonstrates
  repentance. His reply: "Do not extort money from
  anyone by threats or by false accusation, and be content with your wages" (v. 14).
- In *1 Timothy 6* Paul warns the young Timothy about
  false teachers. Not only do they teach false doc-
  trines, but they are also greedy, holding to the wrong
  idea that godliness is a way to become wealthy. Paul

responds, saying, "godliness with contentment is great gain, for we brought nothing into the world, and we cannot take anything out of the world. But if we have food and clothing, with these we will be content" (6–8).

• Near the end of the book of Hebrews the author gives several general commands about the Christian life including this: "Keep your life free from love of money, and be content with what you have, for he has said, 'I will never leave you nor forsake you'" (13:5, quoting from Deuteronomy 31:6–8).

As this last passage reminds us, contentment is not about some abstract philosophy. Instead it is very personal; it is based on the character and promises of God and on our relationship to Him as His children. God has loved us in such an astounding way that He gave His own Son for us (Romans 8:32). Certainly He will also give us lesser things, such as food and clothing. He makes the wealthy and the poor (1 Samuel 2:7). If we have the power to make wealth, that power comes from Him (Deuteronomy 8:18). As He cares for cattle (Psalm 104:14) and for birds (Luke 12:24), so He will care for us (Matthew 6:30). He is pleased to richly bless us with things to enjoy (1 Timothy 6:17). But possessions do not determine the quality of our service for God. If we are poor, we can be rich in faith (James 2:5). If we are wealthy, we can be rich in generosity (1 Timothy 6:18).

CONTENTMENT AND HARD WORK

When I teach about contentment I often get two questions. The first goes like this: "Well, if I'm content, does that mean I just sit around and do nothing?" The answer is, "Not at all." Contentment does not mean laziness. The same Paul who taught contentment worked very hard at two jobs: church planting and tent making. In 2 Thessalonians 3 he reminds that church that when he was with them he could have accepted financial support but instead he "worked night and day" so that he might not burden them (v. 8). He put himself forward as an example to follow (v. 9). He closes the section saying, "For even when we were with you, we would give you this command: If anyone is not willing to work, let him not eat" (v. 10).

In Colossians 3:23–24 Paul has a similar perspective on work. The issue is working hard to take care of myself, to care for others who need me or depend on me (e.g., 1 Timothy 5:8; Ephesians 4:28), and to give to ministry (1 Timothy 5:17–18).

CONTENTMENT AND WEALTH

The second question I often hear regards Christians and wealth. "Is it okay to be wealthy?" The short answer is yes. Under the old covenant, the obedience of the nation was to lead to the wealth of the nation (Deuteronomy 28:1–8). Godly Christians who were wealthy—or at least better off than most—included Lydia (Acts 16:14), Gaius and Erastus (Romans 16:23), Phoebe (Romans 16:1–2), and Philemon. But we should take seriously Scripture's warnings. Here are two:

Contentment vs. Idolatry: Colossians 3:5 says, "Put to death therefore what is earthly in you: sexual immorality, impurity, passion, evil desire, and covetousness, which is idolatry" (compare Ephesians 5:5). While in the Old Testament idolatry has to do with the worship of images and of false gods such as Dagon, Ashera, and Baal, in the New Testament idolatry has taken on a wider meaning. Greed displays a fundamental distortion of reality. When we are covetous we place enjoyment, longing, and trust in something (money, financial power) that should only be directed to God. Money becomes what we trust to take care of us.

Contentment vs. Deceitful Money: In His parable of the soils, Jesus describes the seed sown among thorns as "the one who hears the word, but the cares of the world and the deceitfulness of riches choke the word, and it proves unfruitful" (Matthew 13:22). How do riches deceive? They promise peace and security but cannot give it. For, as Proverbs 23:4–5 say, "Do not toil to acquire wealth; be discerning enough to desist. When your eyes light on it, it is gone, for suddenly it sprouts wings, flying like an eagle toward heaven." Similarly, Psalm 62:10 warns, "if riches increase, set not your heart on them."

OUR LONGING OF DISCONTENT

The second virtue of our chapter is discontented longing. That may seem strange, that we have a longing characterized by discontent. But the suffering that typifies the present and the assured hope of the future bring about this discontented longing. The apostle Paul alludes to this discontent in Romans 8:

> The Spirit himself bears witness with our spirit that we are children of God, and if children, then heirs—heirs of God and fellow heirs with Christ, provided we suffer with him in order that we may also be glorified with him. For I consider that the sufferings of this present time are not worth comparing with the glory that is to be revealed to us. For the creation waits with eager longing for the revealing of the sons of God. For the creation was subjected to futility, not willingly, but because of him who subjected it, in hope that the creation itself will be set free from its bondage to corruption and obtain the

freedom of the glory of the children of God. For we know
that the whole creation has been groaning together in the
pains of childbirth until now. And not only the creation,
but we ourselves, who have the firstfruits of the Spirit,
groan inwardly as we wait eagerly for adoption as sons,
the redemption of our bodies. (vv. 16–23)

In the beginning of Romans 8 Paul presents several glorious
and encouraging truths: the law of the Spirit has set us free (v. 2),
Christ dwells in us (v. 10), we have God's Holy Spirit (v. 9), and we
are adopted as God's children (v. 15). This is all immensely positive.

With verse 17 Paul alerts us to a challenge in our lives: While
the future holds out glory, in the current age we suffer. So Paul has
set out a tension: great future expectation and present pain. This
is where the discontented longing—and a groaning—come in.

THIS GROANING wants to leave sin and
frustration—it is discontented with the way
the world is. It longs for something better.

This groaning is a physical manifestation of an emotion. But
the emotion is based on convictions about theology and about history. On the one hand this groaning wants to leave sin and frustration—it is discontented with the way the world is. It wants, on
the other hand, to receive the glorious future that God has promised—it longs for something better. Both we and creation groan.

The Groaning of Creation. We find Paul treating creation as if it had a personality: "creation waits with eager longing" (v. 19). When he does this, he has much in common with the Old Testament writers who spoke of creation rejoicing over God's care or mourning over human sin (for example Psalm 65:12–13; Isaiah 24:4; Jeremiah 4:28, 12:4; Hosea 4:1–3). The creation has been subjected to frustration (Romans 8:20). The frustration comes from not being able to carry out fully what it was designed to do: provide for all humans' need to thrive. Instead, because of the curse of Genesis 3:17, many times creation gives thorns and thistles (or temperatures of 20° below zero!). This groaning is a sign that creation expects something better: a new heaven and a new earth where righteousness—and only righteousness—dwells (2 Peter 3:13; see also Isaiah 65:17–22; Revelation 21:1).

The Groaning of Christians. The key verse is Romans 8:23: "And not only the creation, but we ourselves, who have the first-fruits of the Spirit, groan inwardly as we wait eagerly for adoption as sons, the redemption of our bodies." The word "firstfruit" might strike us as odd, and it really is a term from another world. In an agrarian society the firstfruits were the bit of crop that first came ripe before the main harvest. When firstfruits appeared, they posted a sign that a harvest would soon come. That is, the firstfruits served as a signpost of future hope.

For Christians, the Holy Spirit Himself is the firstfruit (the term is singular and could be translated "the Spirit as firstfruit"). That is, since we have the Holy Spirit as a guarantee (compare 2 Corinthians 5:5), we can be assured that we will have full redemption.

Paul says that we who have the Spirit groan. But what's the relation between having the Spirit and groaning? Because we have the Spirit as firstfruit, [we ourselves] "groan inwardly as we wait eagerly for our adoption," Paul explains (v. 23). So the fruit of the Spirit is joy (Galatians 5:22) *and* because we have the Spirit as the firstfruit, then we groan. Without the Spirit we would not have godly groaning. Without godly groaning we are immature, or unconverted, or perhaps we have squelched Him. We groan as we wait for adoption, that is, the redemption of our body. Paul is not a stoic who thinks the body is evil. The body is not something to be freed from; it just needs to be redeemed. But we see from Romans 8 two things that, on the surface, look contradictory. On the one hand, we have already been adopted as God's children. Because we have the Spirit we cry "Abba, Father!" (Romans 8:15). But adoption is not a wholly past event; we still await our full adoption/redemption.

Paul gives this same perspective in 2 Corinthians 5:1–5:

> For we know that if the tent that is our earthly home is destroyed, we have a building from God, a house not made with hands, eternal in the heavens. For in this tent we groan, longing to put on our heavenly dwelling, if indeed by putting it on we may not be found naked. For while we are still in this tent, we groan, being burdened—not that we would be unclothed, but that we would be further clothed, so that what is mortal may be swallowed up by life. He who has prepared us for this very thing is God, who has given us the Spirit as a guarantee.

We see that the Holy Spirit is linked to groaning. Groaning might seem like a negative emotion, but it is actually linked to a mature attitude toward our current existence. This is a longing for restoration that God has promised for us.

HOW DO WE GROAN?

This groaning for restoration and our redeemed bodies is not to be confused with the discouragement, depression, or anxiety of our age. It is not suicidal. It is motivated not only by the avoidance of pain but by the hope of obtaining the fullness of what God has promised. This groaning is to an extent passive: we await the completion of God's grace. While it is good to work toward making the world a better place for every human being, we must confess that in the final analysis only the intervention of God will make things right.

In our individual lives we might groan in a great variety of ways. We know the evil of our own hearts; often we struggle with the same sinful habits over and over again. We might long for sinlessness. Even with our best of intentions we experience pain in relationships and long for a time when we do not hurt others, when we are not misunderstood by those we love. Others of us might be weighed down with illness. We long for the new body God has promised (2 Corinthians 5; Philippians 3:21) and an eternal home with no pain and mourning (Revelation 21:4).

Still others are glad to have a job. We find some satisfaction in using the skills God has given us. Yet at times the tasks are tedious, or they are taxing—the "sweat of the brow" (Genesis 3:19 NIV) sets in at times. We are fatigued. We long for rest. We also await a time of redemption—deliverance to a perfect kingdom where work is no longer necessary and we experience life eternal and free of pain.

THE SUM OF OUR FEELINGS

In the New Testament, contentment has to do with a person's perspective on money and possessions (Luke 3:14; Philippians 4:10–13; 1 Timothy 6:6–8; Hebrews 13:5). No matter how much or how little money I have, it is a cause for neither anxiety nor arrogance. And that's where it ends. Contentment has nothing to do with other areas of life. So, for instance, I can trust God with the salvation of my neighbors and family, but I should not be "content" if they reject the gospel. Rather, their rejection ought to pain me; this pain should lead me to be diligent in prayer for them.

In contrast, the same Paul who teaches so clearly on contentment also says that believers groan because they have the Holy Spirit. This groaning is a holy discontent and longing. The Spirit works in us, so we long for final redemption (Romans 8:21–23). In other words, "feeling not okay" with this life is a godly virtue. For, with a holy longing, we look forward to the completion of our redemption. There is a caution here: If I do not have such a longing, then an eternal home where righteousness dwells means nothing to me; instead, I have become satisfied with life on a sin-filled planet. Yes, a holy discontent should be part of our emotional life.

Toward a Healthy Emotional Life

Thanksgiving should be a regular part of our prayers—indeed, a regular part of daily life. Thankfulness feeds our sense of contentment. Here are several ways to develop an attitude of contentment even as we live with an appropriate discontented longing for our final redemption.

1. *Keep a journal with a list of things you are thankful for.* Try to add to the list daily or at least weekly.

2. *Read blogs or newsletters from missionaries, from church planters, and from organizations* such as The Voice of the Martyrs (http://www.persecution.com). While your own economic stress might continue, it will look different compared to the lives of others.

3. *Reread Romans 8:17–39.* Pray and ask God to reveal ways you ought to be groaning.

4. *Ponder the glories and joys of Revelation 5 and 21; pray through Philippians 1:18–21.* In both, ask God to give you a longing for your eternal home.

Questions for Discussion

1. How did you define contentment before reading this chapter? How does that definition compare to, or contrast with, the definition given here?
2. Read Ephesians 5:5 and Colossians 3:5. Explain in your own words how Paul can call greed idolatry. Since greed is idolatry, what other sins can be idolatrous? Explain.

3. The author asserts that the fruit of the Spirit is joy (and that joy has emotional content) and that the Spirit produces in us godly groaning. Explain how, in your view, joy and groaning can go together.

4. Evaluate this statement: "If I do not have a longing for heaven, then an eternal home where righteousness dwells means nothing to me; instead, I have become satisfied with life on a sin-filled planet."

5. In your own life, in what areas should you be more content? In what areas should you be groaning more?

Suggestions for Further Reading

Alcorn, Randy. *Heaven*. Carol Stream, IL: Tyndale, 2004.

Witherington, Ben. *Jesus and Money*. Grand Rapids: Brazos, 2010.

10 ◆ The Loss of *Sadness*

MY GREAT GRANDFATHER was a Methodist circuit rider. Perhaps before going further you want to ask, What's a circuit rider? It has nothing to do with big box electronic stores.

This was the early 1900s in central Florida, and circuit riders like my grandfather rode a horse between villages to preach in little churches. At the time, those villages were just the beginning of settlements in central Florida, now the home to booming suburban developments, water parks, and amusement attractions like Disney World and Universal Studios. He did much good there preaching the gospel over and over again and working with congregations. A devout man, he lived to be ninety-five years old.

But there was a problem: he was a hard man. He was deeply religious, deeply spiritual, and very committed to the gospel, but he was emotionally distant. If he displayed one emotion, it was anger. Because of his emotional distance, I had a problem getting to know him. I got to know him somewhat during times together when I was six, seven, and eight years old. Of course, I did not have much theological acumen then, and we could not engage in lengthy spiritual conversations.

I could imagine what a conversation would be like if I were to talk to him now. I might say something like this:

"Grandpa, you're hard to get to know."

"There is nothing wrong with that. God is hard to get to know."

"You don't seem very happy."

"Scripture says nothing about happiness; it says we should be sober minded."

"And I never see you cry."

"Of course not. Scripture says, 'Rejoice in the Lord always.'"

"But you seem angry. Aren't you angry?"

"No, I'm not angry because Scripture says, 'The anger of man does not accomplish the righteousness of God.'"

You can see that getting to know this guy would be like pulling teeth. From his perspective, being so hard to reach was a good thing. If other people didn't like it, that was their problem, not his.

My stepfather was not much different. I saw him cry once. It was a strange thing. I was maybe six or seven years old. Near the end of my mom's short marriage to my stepfather, we met in the den one day. He was crying and saying that my mom, my sister, and I were going to go live with my grandmother. We would be there awhile and then he was going to come be with us. Unfortunately I learned later that this promise was not true. They were divorcing and they were not willing to come right out and say it. So in my two or three years with my stepfather I never had an emotional connection with him until he was weeping over losing us. Maybe it would have been good to see him cry over something else, like a movie or something. I really wanted more time with him, to know him and to learn, eventually, that men and boys can cry.

What was the result of these experiences? I grew up being a stoic. I learned that one should not be overly happy; that is bad. No kind of emotional reaction was good if it was too much on one side. You are allowed to be mildly perturbed, not allowed to be too angry; that is bad. Not allowed to cry; that is bad. So I grew up thinking people have to be very careful to go right down the middle of the rails and not be too emotional on one side or the other.

In some ways, twenty-first-century society is similar. American adults hate sadness. They prefer to be angry or to have a shallow cheerfulness—anything to avoid feeling sad!

WHAT IS SADNESS?

To be sad is to be affected by unhappiness or grief; to be sorrowful or mournful. Often it is attached to loss (so we might call it grief). Sadness might come on us because of lost goals, lost relationships, lost health, or the loss of loved ones by death. We might describe it as feeling blue, being discouraged or depressed. Other words for the feeling include gloomy, dispirited, downcast, dejected, dismayed, or even feeling numb.

Sadness might feel like we have become closed in or that our world has become dark. It is a hurt that is not the pain of a cut or broken bone; it is the hurt in the mind and heart. While it is sometimes the case that sadness becomes so severe that it needs professional treatment (such as counseling or medication), we are so afraid of sadness lingering that we are too quick to "treat" it rather than work through it and learn from it.

Normal sadness includes a few different aspects. First, as noted above, it happens because of some loss in life, such as of a job, a cherished goal, or a lingering illness of a beloved. Second, its intensity is in proportion to the loss suffered. Appropriate sadness involves perceiving reality properly and having an appropriate emotional reaction. If I go into a lengthy depression because I have lost my favorite pet rock, you would rightly say that my sorrow is out of proportion with my loss. On the other hand, it may take months or years for one to recover from the loss of a child or spouse.

Third, normal sorrow tends to dissipate with time, especially if the thing that triggered my sorrow goes away. Or I might learn to adapt to new conditions and so find that I gradually emerge from the sadness. However, as academics Allan Horowitz and Jerome Wakefield write, "As long as stressful environments persist, symptoms can also be long-standing. Sadness endures in contexts such as troubled marriages, oppressive jobs, persistent poverty, or chronic illness because the stressful circumstances that produced it remain unchanged."[1]

SADNESS'S INTENSITY is in proportion to the loss suffered. It may take years to recover from the loss of a child or spouse.

Often sadness is the result of love. If someone dear to us dies we grieve. Lack of grief tells all around us that there was a lack of love, since "grief cannot be excluded from the good life even if it is one of the most painful and devastating emotions. If loving and caring are essential to life, then so is grief, which is nothing less than the realization of our extreme vulnerability to loss."[2]

Knowing that our loved one was a Christian and so will live in the new heaven and new earth (Revelation 21:1) might lessen our grief. But it will not take it away. What will take our grief away is changing the deceased person from someone we love to someone we do not love. A rock, an island, a person who lives not in a community but as an independent human being—such a thing cannot exist—is the person who feels no grief.

Since many godly people have suffered sadness, we need to ask if sadness has a place among Christian virtuous emotions. I think it does. Let's start by looking to Jesus.

A LOOK AT JESUS' GRIEF

On two known occasions, Jesus grieves. Perhaps the more amazing display of tears, however, occurs shortly after what many would consider His greatest acclamation, His triumphal entry into Jerusalem. "As he was drawing near—already on the way down the Mount of Olives—the whole multitude of his disciples began to rejoice and praise God with a loud voice for all the mighty works that they had seen, saying, 'Blessed is the King who comes in the name of the Lord! Peace in heaven and glory in the highest!'" (Luke 19:37–38).

This happens a week before Jesus dies. He has been traveling all over Galilee and Judea for three years doing ministry and now, near the end of life, He is coming back into Jerusalem. Since it is Passover Week, people are getting ready for the festival and crowds are coming into the city. Matthew, Mark, Luke, and John all tell this story and they all tell it a little differently; however, we know that this event happened only once. So the unique features of any gospel writer's particular telling of the event let us in on his particular concerns. Only in Luke's recording of this story do you find these words: "the crowd rejoiced," "praise God," "loud voice," "all the mighty works they had seen," and "peace . . . glory."

Luke presents this event as even happier than all the other gospels make this event. Something is coming later, however, something to contrast this happiness. At this point Luke is setting us up. He wants us to see it as a happy event, an exciting time, so that what happens next strikes us.

What happens next is the theological police show up: The Pharisees disapprove. "Some of the Pharisees in the crowd said to him, 'Teacher, rebuke your disciples'" (v. 39). Either they are thinking that this is a bit too happy, or they think there is really no reason to be happy at all. It is as if the Pharisees are saying,

"Jesus, all these people are praising you as if you are somebody special and we, the specialists in the law, know that you are not. So if you are really a good teacher, you ought to correct them." There have got to be party poopers at every party and here they are. The Pharisees are giving this really negative response. What will Jesus say?

Jesus affirms that His entry into Jerusalem is a joyful event. "He answered, 'I tell you, if these were silent, the very stones would cry out'" (v. 40). This *is* a happy time. Somebody has got to praise! Somebody has got to rejoice! Somebody has got to speak glory, and if these people do not do it, someone else will! Jesus says this situation is so glorious that even the stones could cry out. The ironic thing about this is that lifeless things know life when they see it. But those who have a sort of life do not know life when they see it. The Pharisees cannot recognize life, but rocks can.

IN THE MIDST OF such a joyful situation, why does Jesus suddenly cry?

Jesus affirms that this entry into Jerusalem is a great thing. The crowd realizes this is a great situation, but Luke is setting us up for some disappointment here. It comes at verse 41: "And when he drew near and saw the city, he wept over it."

Wait a minute! I thought this situation was supposed to be really happy; I thought the situation was supposed to be absolutely fantastic. Luke wants us to get to verse 41 and say, "What?! This just does not make any sense."

Of course, this is the way that any good story works—the writer presents elements of the story in a way that brings you to a point where you are shocked. Now you really pay attention; all of a sudden we see that what is going on is not what we expected. In the midst of such a joyful situation, why does Jesus suddenly cry? This is one of two places in the Gospels where Jesus is said to cry (the other is John 11:35). So we should look carefully for the reason. He begins to tell us in verse 42. He wept, saying:

> Would that you, even you, had known on this day the things that make for peace! But now they are hidden from your eyes. For the days will come upon you, when your enemies will set up a barricade around you and surround you and hem you in on every side and tear you down to the ground, you and your children within you. And they will not leave one stone upon another in you, because you did not know the time of your visitation.

Jerusalem—the holy city, God's chosen city—is filled with people who ought to know God and live in righteousness. But Jerusalem's residents are ignorant. Ignorant of things that make for peace; that is, they do not know that Jesus brings peace. This ignorance means judgment is coming.

An army is going to surround them. (This actually happens in AD 70.) The Romans come and for seven months they laid siege on Jerusalem. They surround the walled city and no one can come in nor go out. No food or water, and after seven months there is cannibalism in the city. It is horrifying. This takes place some forty years or so after Jesus' death and resurrection, but He knows it is coming. He can foresee this and He weeps over their ignorance and their coming judgment. It is just amazing.

ABOUT JESUS' TEARS

What do we learn from these tears wept over Jerusalem? Let me mention two truths about Jesus.

First, Jesus is hurt to see people facing wrath, even when this wrath is decades away, and even when this wrath is deserved. Jerusalem rejects its Messiah. Jesus Himself said, "O Jerusalem, Jerusalem, the city that kills the prophets and stones those who are sent to it! How often would I have gathered your children together as a hen gathers her brood under her wings, and you were not willing! Behold, your house is forsaken. And I tell you, you will not see me until you say, 'Blessed is he who comes in the name of the Lord!'" (Luke 13:34–35).

So even though Jerusalem deserves the wrath that Jesus describes in Luke 19:42–44, He still weeps over the prospect. The Lord Jesus, to whom all judgment has been given (John 5:22), is not emotionally detached in His judgment. He is not only angry; He can also weep over coming judgment.

Second, Jesus experiences pain over this broken relationship. He wants a relationship with people. Describing His mission, the Lord says, "For the Son of Man came to seek and to save the lost" (Luke 19:10). When the relationship is broken or when people refuse His message, it hurts Him. Jesus' pain is not always at the surface; there are times when He rejoices (Luke 10:21). There are other times, however, when human hard-heartedness, weakness, or sin strike Him as painful (Mark 1:41, 3:5; John 11:38).

QUESTIONS WE SHOULD ASK OURSELVES

We should ask ourselves three questions in response to Jesus' words of sadness and warning. First, do we think that knowledge of the future will keep us from pain? I suspect we do. Sometimes students come into the office to talk about decisions concerning their future, especially deciding whom to marry. The conversation might go like this:

"How can I make sure that I marry the right woman or the right guy? I just have to make sure I marry the exact right person. I am worried that I might marry the wrong person."

"Why are you worried?"

"Well, I do not want to disobey God. If I marry the wrong person, that would be really bad."

"Yes, I suppose that it could be bad. Can you explain more about what worries you?"

"You know, like, if I marry the wrong person it could be hard and painful."

"And if you marry the right person, then everything about your marriage will be painless and happy; is that what you mean?"

"Well . . . uh . . . I guess not."

"You see, even if God wrote the name of your spouse in the sky so that you could be sure you marry the 'right' person, there would still be times of both joy and pain in your marriage. Even perfect, Godlike knowledge will not keep your marriage from hard times."

I wonder if sometimes we think, "If I just had better knowledge of the future I could avoid pain." Jesus could not do that. Why is He weeping? He weeps because He knows the future; He knows it quite well; He knows exactly what is going to happen. Jerusalem is going to be flattened by Rome. Knowledge of the future—even omniscient knowledge of the future—is not saving Him from pain. It will not save us either.

Second, do we sometimes think that trusting God as we should will mean that we are serene, calm, and tranquil? Jesus does command, "Do not be anxious about tomorrow, for tomorrow will be anxious for itself" (Matthew 6:34). Do we take this to mean that Jesus forbids us from having any negative emotions about future events? If we answer yes, such an approach to life owes more to stoic philosophy than it does to Scripture. If we remember that Jesus never sinned (2 Corinthians 5:21), we must draw the conclusion that He always trusted His Father as He should. But this trust—this perfect trust—did not keep Him from feeling pain, even pain about future events.

JESUS ALWAYS trusted His Father, as He should. But this perfect trust did not keep Him from feeling pain.

One of the great privileges of working at Moody Bible Institute is the opportunity to teach a course called Biblical Theology of Suffering. In the course we talk about painful emotions such as anger, depression, and fear. Often we have a few students in the course who have grown up in churches that are doing exactly to them what my great grandfather did to me. "Do not be anything but emotionally centered," they have been told. "If you have too much joy"—please forgive the expression; this is what is given to me by my students in class—"then you are a charismatic." Gasp! Any emotional response is awful. Do not do that!

The same students must rule out anger and sadness. If you are angry that is a sin, because Scripture says the anger of man does not accomplish the righteousness of God (James 1:20). Cry? You are not allowed to cry. After all, Scripture gives this commandment, "Rejoice in the Lord always" (Philippians 4:4). How dare you cry?

I was at the coffee shop one morning when I overheard a conversation among six ladies who are obviously Christians. They were talking about discipleship, church, Bible study, and small groups. One of them said, "I only have anxiety and cry because I do not trust God."

Perhaps she is among the many who have grown up in homes or in churches that basically tell us we need to be emotionally centered. We think that trusting God wholeheartedly means being tranquil. But the truth is that such a view of our emotions makes life flat, two-dimensional, instead of robust as it should be. Further, I think we can have anxiety while we trust Him. I suspect, however, that some readers will think that it just will not—and should not—happen.

Third, we should ask ourselves this: How do we react when people get what they deserve?

This is a hard question. How do you react when people get what they deserve? Perhaps you know a Christian woman preparing to marry a non-Christian man and you warn her, "Do not marry him. The Bible says that we should not be unequally yoked together with nonbelievers" (2 Corinthians 6:14). But she marries him anyway, it is a painful life, and they divorce later. What do you say? "I told you so"? That is not Jesus' response.

Suppose you know two men who engage in sex together and they get HIV. What is your response? "You deserve this; this is just the wrath of God against you." I doubt this is Jesus' response.

Suppose this summer you take a trip downtown and you meet someone homeless on the street who tells you, "Well I did a couple years in prison for dealing drugs, and when I got out I tried to rent a room but my roommates stole all my stuff and kicked me out. Now I am homeless." Your response is, "You did this to yourself. Sorry." That is not Jesus' response. Suppose your dad's liver is failing and now he's in the hospital because he is drinking himself to death. Is your reaction bitter indifference? That is not Jesus' response. No, in all these cases, Jesus would weep over their rebellion and their loss, just as He did for the people of Jerusalem who turned against Him. The judgment coming on Jerusalem is deserved. Jesus knows that better than anyone and He weeps over it.

I have to admit it is easy for me to be bitter and indifferent when people get what they deserve, but don't we *all* deserve hell anyway? It is good for us *not* to get what we deserve. Hopefully no one else is bitter about it. John Piper has an excellent sermon on this passage in which he says, "If the sovereign Christ weeps how can we, his followers, be hard-hearted?"[3] It's a good question.

"I NOW TELL YOU WITH TEARS"

If Jesus can experience sadness, then so can other godly people. Here are a few examples, from Abraham to Paul the apostle, of those who allowed their tears to flow in sadness:

- When "Sarah died at Kiriath-arba (that is, Hebron) in the land of Canaan, . . . Abraham went in to mourn for Sarah and to weep for her" (Genesis 23:2). The death of a beloved spouse is especially painful.
- One of the sons of Korah is in distress. He is not hesitant to be honest about his feelings. He writes, "My tears have been my food day and night, while they say to me all the day long, "Where is your God?" (Psalm 42:3).
- Hannah had been married to Elkanah for many years, and yet they had no children. Infertility was a source of great pain and disappointment for her. The Scripture says, "She was deeply distressed and prayed to

the Lord and wept bitterly" (1 Samuel 1:10).

• Jeremiah's ministry was often painful, since he preached the coming judgment on Israel for its sin. How did he feel about this? "Oh that my head were waters, and my eyes a fountain of tears, that I might weep day and night for the slain of the daughter of my people!" (Jeremiah 9:1).

• In Philippians, the letter known for its note of joy, the apostle Paul says, "Brothers, join in imitating me, and keep your eyes on those who walk according to the example you have in us. For many, of whom I have often told you and now tell you even with tears, walk as enemies of the cross of Christ. Their end is destruction, their god is their belly, and they glory in their shame, with minds set on earthly things" (Philippians 3:17–19). Paul, like Jesus, weeps over those who get the judgment they deserve.

In chapter 3 we looked briefly at Romans 12:15: "Rejoice with those who rejoice, weep with those who weep" in terms of rejoicing. But this command also tells us we should recognize those who are sad or in grief and share in their feelings. This is empathy. We need not be uncomfortable shedding tears with those who are grieving.

In 1997 I served as pastor of a small church in south central Iowa. One day I was in the church "office"—the basement of my house—when I got a telephone call that Grandpa Jones had died. The Jones family were members of our church. The son of Grandpa Jones was a welder; his wife held daycare services in their home. They had two sons, one in junior high and one in high school. I taught the high school boy how to drive a stick shift in the parking lot of the grocery store; it was a lot of fun.

So I got a call that Grandpa had died. They told me that I should come right away. I have to admit that the first thing that came to my mind was, "I am going to mess this up. I am going to go there and there will be all these people around dead Grandpa and I am going to say something stupid and I am going to look even stupider."

I got there; my heart was racing and I was very nervous. I entered the room and there was the new widow, the son, the wife of the son and their two children and another cousin. There were about seven or eight people all standing around Grandpa now that he had died. I walked in there and they all had this deer-in-the-headlights look. They did not know what to do. They were just standing there like they were in shock. It was dead quiet. I walked in and they all looked at me. *No, do not look at me!* I thought. *Man, I am really going to mess this up.*

For about fifteen seconds I did not know what to say, so I was just standing there. Then I thought that if I were to pray at least their eyes will be closed so they will not be able to see me.

So I walked over to Grandpa, put my hand on his shoulder, and said, "Let's pray." I started praying whatever came to mind—I don't remember—and after about fifteen seconds I started crying. I do not know why. But I managed to get through the rest of the prayer, which took about a minute, and I ended with, "Amen." When I said, "Amen," everybody started crying and hugging each other. Now I knew that I had been a little bit of help to be there. I had given them all permission to weep, to grieve. They grieved and tears came, and I grieved with them.

WHAT IS UNGODLY SORROW AND GRIEF?

Romans 12:15 makes clear we are to "weep with those who weep." So we know that some sorrow, some sadness and grief, is godly. But of course, not all of it is. Let's look at some examples of ungodly grief.

Because we are sinners, there will be times when we experience ungodly sorrow. Ungodly sorrow occurs when we have envy, jealousy, selfishness, greed, bitterness, or similar emotions and perspectives toward people or situations. When we interpret our world as causing us to suffer loss, it is common to have sorrow or grief. But sometimes the loss is of something we should not have.

Here are two telling examples of ungodly grief, one found in the Old Testament, the other in the New. The judge Samson disobeyed his parents and God when he chose to marry a Philistine woman (Judges 14:1–3). During the weeklong wedding feast, he proposed a riddle to the Philistine young men. Attached to solving the riddle was a wager. When they could not solve it, they pressured Samson's wife to find the answer. He resisted telling her.

The passage says, "And Samson's wife wept over him and said, 'You only hate me; you do not love me. You have put a riddle to my people, and you have not told me what it is.' And he said to her, 'Behold, I have not told my father nor my mother, and shall I tell you?' She wept before him the seven days that their feast lasted, and on the seventh day he told her, because she pressed him hard. Then she told the riddle to her people" (vv. 16–17). These are not tears of godly grief but selfish manipulation.

Revelation 18 tells of the final destruction of Babylon—the literal city on the Euphrates River—and its greed, luxury, and other sins that were heaped as high as heaven (v. 5). When it is destroyed, what is the reaction?

The merchants of the earth weep and mourn for her, since no one buys their cargo anymore, cargo of gold, silver, jewels, pearls, fine linen, purple cloth, silk, scarlet

cloth, all kinds of scented wood, all kinds of articles of
ivory, all kinds of articles of costly wood, bronze, iron and
marble, cinnamon, spice, incense, myrrh, frankincense,
wine, oil, fine flour, wheat, cattle and sheep, horses and
chariots, and slaves, that is, human souls. "The fruit for
which your soul longed has gone from you, and all your
delicacies and your splendors are lost to you, never to be
found again!" The merchants of these wares, who gained
wealth from her, will stand far off, in fear of her torment,
weeping and mourning aloud. (vv. 11–15)

This is not godly grief but mourning because of loss of power,
of luxury, of exploitation.

Ungodly grief can happen to those who follow God but fall
into selfish patterns or self-centered goals. For me, such ungodly
grief happened when, over a decade ago, I was pastoring a small
church plant in central Florida. It was my first job in full-time
ministry, and after a few months it became clear that the church
was going to close. Many Mondays I wept over this. But the more
I prayed and pondered over my grief, the more it became clear
that I was sad about *my* being a failure. The grief was not about
the people, our witness to the community, nor the glory of God.
It was about the loss of my own goal of being successful. That is
not godly grief but selfish grief.

THE SUM OF OUR FEELINGS

If we have goals, especially goals that are precious to us, then
we will sometimes have sorrow. We can't get everything we want
in this world. Even omniscient knowledge of a blessed and happy
future will not keep us from such grief. Similarly if we love, we
will grieve, for sooner or later a loved one will die. Knowledge

that the loved one is in heaven might lessen the grief, but it need not take it all away. Such grief is not only normal—since Jesus Himself grieved, such grief is godly.

Toward a Healthy Emotional Life

1. *Allow yourself to be sad.* Denying such feelings may force them underground, where they can do more damage with time. *Let your tears flow.* Tears are one normal way of displaying sadness, so do not conclude that crying is immature or ungodly. Many people find that the intensity of their sadness or distress lessens after crying. This sense of relief might come about because crying is an exocrine process, such as exhaling, where the body releases chemicals that are produced in us by stress.

2. *Bring your sadness to God in prayer.* We do not always know the working of our own heart, so all sadness should be brought to God in prayer, asking Him to help us see what its causes and goals are. He is the one who can search and know our hearts, discerning if there is some harmful pattern in us (Psalm 139:22–23). Remember, some sadness (or grief) is good (the continued unbelief of a neighbor), but some can be selfish (falling behind in the economic competition with the same neighbor). Through prayer, pondering, and godly counsel we might find that many of our griefs are selfish or manipulative. If so, we need repentance and a transfer of affections. Recall my tears over the closing of the church in Florida. After realizing what was going on in my own heart, I needed to repent of my desire to be seen as successful. I needed to set my affections on people, on the advance of the gospel, and on the glory of God.

3. *Be alert to any long-term sadness and ready to seek assistance if necessary.* Depression is common in our age. Be wary of any prolonged sadness if it leads to the inability to love and

to carry out normal responsibilities. In such cases there is no shame in getting professional help from pastors, counselors, physicians, or psychiatrists, or a combination of these professionals. We are complex creatures, and recovering from prolonged sadness may well require treatment of body, mind, habits, and relationships.

4. *Help others who are feeling sadness.* One of the best ways to help others is to obey the Bible command to "weep with those who weep" (Romans 12:15). This is empathy, mentioned earlier in the chapter. Shed tears with them. In your mourning, you will show empathy and compassion. Remember, sometimes to imitate Jesus means just crying.

Questions for Discussion

1. Evaluate this statement: "Sadness is normal."
2. Do you think that knowledge of the future will keep you from pain? Explain your answer.
3. The judgment coming on Jerusalem was deserved. Jesus knew that better than anyone and yet He wept over it. How do you react when people get what they deserve?
4. From your own life, give an example of godly sorrow and of ungodly sorrow.
5. Evaluate this statement: "Christians shouldn't be sad because it will hinder their witness for Christ."
6. How are you doing with the command of Romans 12:15: "Weep with those who weep"?

Suggestions for Further Reading

Allender, Dan and Tremper Longman III. *The Cry of the Soul.* Colorado Springs: NavPress, 1994.

Horowitz, Allan V. and Jerome C. Wakefield. *The Loss of Sadness.* New York: Oxford University Press, 2007.

Lewis, C. S. *A Grief Observed.* New York: Harper Collins, 2001.

11 ◆ Emotions and Spiritual Transformation

IT COMES IN DIFFERENT labels. Some call it *spiritual growth*, others *spiritual formation*, or *sanctification*, or *transformation*. We will be using this last term, since it is Paul's term in the very familiar passage, Romans 12:1–2:

> I appeal to you therefore, brothers, by the mercies of God, to present your bodies as a living sacrifice, holy and acceptable to God, which is your spiritual worship. Do not be conformed to this world, but be transformed by the renewal of your mind, that by testing you may discern what is the will of God, what is good and acceptable and perfect.

Most of us understand we need to be made new. We know well that what we are is not what we should be. We know passages of Scripture that talk about transformation. "We all, with unveiled face, beholding the glory of the Lord, are being transformed into the same image from one degree of glory to another," writes Paul the apostle, who then tells us the source: "For this comes from the Lord who is the Spirit" (2 Corinthians 3:18). Adds Peter: "Grow in the grace and knowledge of our Lord and Savior Jesus Christ. To him be the glory both now and to the day of eternity" (2 Peter 3:18).

But a question arises: How will we know when this is happening? What are the marks of transformation? How will we see it? With a little bit of training, we can spot a termite and distinguish it from an ant. But can we distinguish increased religiosity (or even legalism) from spiritual transformation?

WHAT IS THIS "TRANSFORMATION"?

As with a three-legged stool, transformation has three parts that are essential; if any leg is taken out, the project falls. First, transformation is about beliefs or worldview. We could call this *orthodoxy* (believing in the right theology or right doctrine). Without doubt, correct beliefs are crucial. Second, transformation is about right actions, good decision-making, and good disciplines. The specific term for this is *orthopraxy*—having the right practice or action. Likewise, right action is crucial; James reminds us that "faith apart from works is dead" (2:26). Third, transformation is about the right affections, the right emotions, and the right motivations. We could call this *orthokardia*: having the right heart.

As we've seen, expressing our emotions is essential. But how we express them is also vital. There is a right way to show joy and tears. Anger, love, fear, and the other emotions, all God given, need to be transformed through the power of the Spirit. How do we do that?

We will take a brief look at orthodoxy and orthopraxy, to understand them better and learn how they can fall short. Then we will focus on *orthokardia*, as we learn how we can develop a right heart.

ORTHODOXY: THE FOUNDATION

Belief is foundational. To a large extent Christianity is about belief. One comes into a saving relationship with God by believing the truth of the gospel (Mark 1:15; Romans 5:1). Remember that *orthodoxy* is belief in the right doctrine.

Orthodoxy is related to a proper knowledge of the Scriptures. Thus the apostle Paul commended believers in Thessalonica as he rehearsed to them their conversion to Christ: "We also thank

God constantly for this, that when you received the word of God, which you heard from us, you accepted it not as the word of men but as what it really is, the word of God, which is at work in you believers" (1 Thessalonians 2:13). Orthodoxy is linked to knowledge. Paul prayed for the Colossians that they would "be filled with the knowledge of his will in all spiritual wisdom and understanding, so as to walk in a manner worthy of the Lord, fully pleasing to him, bearing fruit in every good work and increasing in the knowledge of God" (Colossians 1:9–10).

Belief and worldview are closely related. We can have a hodgepodge of different Christian beliefs that do not form a coherent view of the world. There can be various aspects of this worldview change:

- *In our goals* ("to do my job well as evidence of faith"; "to minister to other people in order to bring them into this family of faith").
- *In our personal values and attitudes* ("I want to be a good Christian").
- *In one's self-definition and identity* ("before I was a Jew, now I am a Christian").
- *In our life purpose* ("to fulfill God's mission").
- *In a revised life story* that highlights how an important turning point has had positive consequences for one's story ("I see now that God used my bad childhood to make me a stronger person").[1]

These types of changes are good and necessary; all will be affected as we grow. But when our worldview changes, we cannot say that transformation has been fully accomplished. As Jesus pointed out to His disciples, their righteousness must go beyond the righteousness of the scribes and Pharisees (Matthew 5:20).

In many ways the disciples had a proper worldview and proper beliefs and could affirm aspects of the list above. But from the Lord's sharp rebuke of them (e.g., Matthew 23:13–29), we can see that He requires something more than beliefs and worldview, something hidden in the heart of a person (Matthew 5:8). Our emotions and motivations need to change as well.

Such a call to transformation must be part of Jesus' parable of the Good Samaritan. Jesus tells of a man walking from Jerusalem to Jericho being surrounded by robbers, "who stripped him and beat him and departed, leaving him half dead" (Luke 10:30). First a priest and then a Levite traveled that road. Each saw the victim, but neither helped him; they passed by on the other side (10:31). The Samaritan saw, stopped, and helped.

What made the Samaritan different? "He had compassion" (Luke 10:33). Therefore I fall short of transformation if my affections have not changed. What I love, what I long for, what unspoken motivations I have, my capacity to love gladly and sacrificially—these things might not change even if my worldview changes.

Our orthodoxy will know that the two greatest commands of Scripture are to love God and to love our neighbor (Matthew 22:36–39). Our orthodoxy might even know that these loves contain an affective or emotional element (see chapter 7). But then, how do we develop these affections?

ORTHOPRAXY: ACTION AND DECISION

Part of transformation is action and decision. This is orthopraxy. We should be in the process of learning to make the best choices, as in the prayer that Paul prayed for the Philippians: "I pray that your love will keep on growing and that you will fully know and understand how to make the right choices. Then you will still be pure and innocent when Christ returns" (1:9–10 CEV). Similarly his prayer for the Colossians asks that they would be "bearing fruit in every good work" (1:10). Yet again, he says that those "who have believed in God" should "be careful to devote themselves to good works" (Titus 3:8). And finally, Paul exhorts Timothy to grow in godliness by way of the Word of God and careful attention to his life (1 Timothy 4:6, 14–16).

Our lives are not just thoughts and beliefs; much in Scripture speaks against mere words or belief without action. As we mentioned in chapter 7, genuine love will be seen in action. The apostle John exhorts his readers, saying,

> By this we know love, that he laid down his life for us, and we ought to lay down our lives for the brothers. But if anyone has the world's goods and sees his brother in need, yet closes his heart against him, how does God's love abide in him? Little children, let us not love in word or talk but in deed and in truth. (1 John 3:16–18)

But there is a potential problem with both orthodoxy and orthopraxy. It is this: what's the motivation? Jesus spoke clearly to this. Is prayer a bad thing? Is fasting ungodly? Is giving money to the poor sinful? The answers: no, no, and no. They are good actions! But the Lord made clear that one might do these actions with the wrong motivation, from the desire to appear generous, spiritual, and godly. Consider these warnings from Jesus delivered during His Sermon on the Mount:

> When you give to the needy, sound no trumpet before you, as the hypocrites do in the synagogues and in the streets, that they may be praised by others. Truly, I say to you, they have received their reward. (Matthew 6:2)

And when you pray, you must not be like the hypocrites. For they love to stand and pray in the synagogues and at the street corners, that they may be seen by others. Truly, I say to you, they have received their reward. (Matthew 6:5)

And when you fast, do not look gloomy like the hypocrites, for they disfigure their faces that their fasting may be seen by others. Truly, I say to you, they have received their reward. (Matthew 6:16)

Christianity is not simply about believing something (orthodoxy) and learning to do something (orthopraxy). Sometimes we need to learn how to deal with the emotional hindrances to doing what we already know we should do and maybe already want to do. So, for instance, pride often interferes with empathy. Fear interferes with love.

ORTHOKARDIA: ISSUES OF THE HEART

This brings us to issues of the heart, or what Jonathan Edwards calls affection. Edwards was probably America's greatest theologian. In 1746 he wrote *A Treatise Concerning Religious Affection* (hereafter called simply *Religious Affection*). For the most part, when Edwards talks about "religion" or something "religious" he means biblical religion, or Christianity; when he talks of "affection" his term is close to what we mean by an emotion, whether a long-term emotion (trait or mood) or a short-term emotion. While not diminishing the significance of orthodoxy and orthopraxy, he says, "True religion, in great part, consists in holy affections."[1] This is *orthokardia*.

As we have said a few times already, we need to ask the question of motivation. What drives our Christian action? For Edwards, the source, the motivation behind Christian action "is very much religious affection." The one who has doctrinal knowledge without religious affections is actually not engaged in Christianity at all.

TRANSFORMING OUR AFFECTIONS

For some of us, the approach of Jonathan Edwards might seem radical, strange, or perhaps even dangerous. We have deeply imbibed the view that transformation includes beliefs, worldview, decision, actions, and choices. And that is where it ends. But there is something more, something that is too often neglected. It is the transformation of affections. It is vital to real Christianity. Edwards states it pointedly:

> For although to true religion there must indeed be something else besides affection; yet true religion consists so much in the affections, that there can be no true religion without them. He who has no religious affection, is in a state of spiritual death, and is wholly destitute of the powerful, quickening, saving influences of the Spirit of God upon his heart. As there is no true religion where there is nothing else but affection, so there is no true religion where there is no religious affection.[2]

"Religious affection" is another phrase for *orthokardia*. We will follow some of the major comments from Edwards, unpacking them a bit and reflecting on Scripture.

Christian Affections Are Motivators to Action. We mentioned this topic briefly in chapter 1. We don't act without motivation. "Such is man's nature," Edwards says, "that he is very inactive, [unless] he is influenced by some affection, either love or hatred, desire, hope, fear, or some other."[3] In all the affairs of our life—

whether it is family, business, job, hobbies, fitness, discipleship, evangelism, service, or worship—it is always some sort of desire or aversion that moves us. When our emotions are intense—we really love something or we really hate something—then we are moved with all the greater intensity to either seek that which we love or avoid that which we hate.

The best motivation is not religious duty; worse yet, hypocrisy. The best motivations are real Christian affections. Among many possibilities, these affections might be love, joy, grief, hatred, fear, or gratitude. So, for instance:

* Love can motivate mercy and forgiveness for others.
* Joy in the gospel can motivate evangelism.
* Grief for sins committed can motivate repentance and struggle to overcome.
* Hatred of evil can motivate prayer to God that His will would be done.
* Fear of the Lord can motivate worship of and obedience to God.
* Gratitude can motivate consistent financial giving.

From this it follows that "wherever true religion is, there are vigorous exercises of the inclination and will towards divine objects: but by what was said before, the vigorous, lively, and sensible exercises of the will, are no other than the affections of the soul."[4]

Christian Affections Are Based on the Character of God. Some of our religious affections will rightly be based in what God has done. We find examples often in the Psalms, where the writer praises or thanks God for rescue from enemies or for help in time of trial (e.g., Psalms 28, 118, 138). For Christians, the greatest source for such affection is the grace shown us in Christ. But there is something more foundational than what God has done.

It is who God is. Edwards puts it this way:

> Indeed the saints rejoice in their interest in God, and that Christ is theirs: and so they have great reason, but this is not the first spring of their joy. They first rejoice in God as glorious and excellent in himself, and then secondarily rejoice in it, that so glorious a God is theirs. They first have their hearts filled with sweetness, from the view of Christ's excellency, and the excellency of his grace and the beauty of the way of salvation by him, and then they have a secondary joy in that so excellent a Savior, and such excellent grace are theirs.[5]

It is similar to seeing an alpine snow-covered mountain. It will strike me as beautiful, powerful, majestic, or even incredible. I am happy to view it; the sight makes me feel small and insignificant. I find it glorious for what it is; but I do not find it glorious for what it does for me. So also with the character of God. We rejoice in who He is in Himself. Who He is, in Himself, humbles us. Who He is, in Himself, fills us with awe and fear.

Christian Affections Are Based on Understanding Scriptural Truth. We have mentioned this several times. It follows from our emotional theory. Our emotions are linked to our beliefs, perspectives, and convictions, whether these are explicit or unconscious. Affections that are not based in Scriptural truth—whether they are positive or negative emotions—cannot be called religious affections (that is, Christian emotions).

Christian Affections Are Strong, not Weak. Too often we save our most intense emotions for that which is small, insignificant, temporary. Too often we have all sorts of emotional energy for work, for a favorite TV show, for sporting events. We have no problem getting excited about an upcoming vacation. When our team wins we can be elated. When we fail to get a raise we can be angry or depressed. We have the emotional capacity; we are just so immature that we are using all our emotional energy on trivial things, while spiritual things get our leftover energy. But that spiritual life that "God requires, and will accept, does not consist in weak, dull, and lifeless wishes, raising us but a little above a state of indifference: God, in His word, greatly insists upon it, that we be good in earnest, 'fervent in spirit,' and our hearts vigorously engaged in religion: Romans 12:11, 'Be fervent in spirit, serving the Lord.'" [6]

WE USE ALL our emotional energy
on trivial things; spiritual things get
our leftover energy.

To drive the point home, Jesus used an illustration from the body. We all know what it means to feel hungry; we know that our body needs nourishment. A hot day in summer can leave us drained and thirsty; we long for a cold drink. These longings arise from deep within; they are just part of being human. A body without hunger and thirst is broken. Thus Jesus says, "Blessed are those who hunger and thirst for righteousness, for they shall be satisfied" (Matthew 5:6). What is the Christianity, the spirituality, that Jesus calls us to? It is one where powerful longings from deep within drive us to seek the holy life that pleases God.

Christian Affections Are Both "Positive" and "Negative." From what we have seen in previous chapters, when we talk about distinctively Christian emotions, we are not talking about continual tranquility and peace. Not all godly affections are positive.

There are some, however, who stress that the transformed life is positive, that what well-being as a Christian means is working to have more and more positive feelings and positive thinking. It means deciding to be optimistic. Along with this goes a reduction in pain, in negative emotions, and in suffering. From this perspective, one of the main solutions to the dilemma of negative feelings is to undo negative emotions by replacing them with positive emotions.

There is a sense in which this is true. Of course we find much rejoicing in Scripture. In chapter 3 (pages 54–55) we wrote, "Joy should be characteristic of our life; it should be our typical experience. This joy will have emotional content; it will be felt. Primarily, this joy will be based on the work that God has already accomplished for us in Christ. Since this Jesus loves us intensely and since He "is the same yesterday and today and forever' (Hebrews 13:8), there is always a reason to rejoice."

BUT THERE ARE problems. Scripture doesn't tell us to get rid of all negative feelings, only certain ones (such as envy).

But there are problems. Scripture doesn't tell us to get rid of all negative feelings, only certain ones (such as envy, Proverbs 3:31; 1 Peter 2:1). In contrast, other negative feelings are encouraged or commanded such as mourning, hatred, and fear

(Romans 12:15; Psalm 97:10; Luke 12:5). When we define spiritual well-being in terms of pleasure (good) versus pain (bad), we have misunderstood Scripture. On this topic Edwards says, in *Religious Affection* (page 33):

> Religious sorrow, mourning, and brokenness of heart, are also frequently spoken of as a great part of true religion. These things are often mentioned as distinguishing qualities of the true saints, and a great part of their character; Matt. 5:4, "Blessed are they that mourn; for they shall be comforted." Psal. 34:18, "The Lord is nigh unto them that are of a broken heart; and saveth such as be of a contrite spirit." Isa. 61:1, 2, "The Lord hath anointed me, to bind up the broken-hearted, to comfort all that mourn." This godly sorrow and brokenness of heart is often spoken of, not only as a great thing in the distinguishing character of the saints, but that in them, which is peculiarly acceptable and pleasing to God; Psal. 51:17, "The sacrifices of God are a broken spirit: a broken and a contrite heart, O God, thou wilt not despise."

My point is not that we be happy all the time. That cannot be. I am talking about something more robust. As a matter of fact, it is not Scripture but our selfishness that will lead us to want to eliminate all negative emotion, for negative emotions do not feel good, so we desire to rid ourselves of them—even though some negative emotion is virtuous (as we saw with Jesus: He wept, He was angry, He had fear).

Furthermore, we find in Scripture truths about God that will lead to a variety of emotional reaction: God is love. We will be delighted. God is a consuming fire. We will be afraid.

LETTING GO OF
NON-CHRISTIAN AFFECTIONS

Cultivating Christian affections can mean letting go of non-Christian affections. In a section that actually deals with Christian practice, Edwards asserts something similar. He says that "a man's actions are the proper trial what a man's heart prefers." He can only truly be said to prefer what he chooses. For instance, there are often times in life when "God and other things stand in competition, God is as it were set before a man on one hand, and his worldly interest or pleasure on the other."[7] Here we face a choice of affections; holding to one prohibits the other.

For instance, my fear might interfere with my generosity. I know that I should give financially to my local church, but I worry that if I give as much as I think I should give, then I will not have enough for my own bills. Here's a negative emotion I need to let go of.

Or again, my pride might get in the way of love. I know I should love. I might even want to love. But pride gets in the way. Let's look at this more closely.

Suppose one day Jill complained to her husband, "You're not listening to me!" Would it be helpful for Jeff to just argue and try to prove that he is listening (like repeating back what she said)? It would be better to ask Jill to clarify, to learn what the comment means. A simple, polite question might lead Jeff to this conclusion: *I am distracted when she talks to me; I do not focus, but instead my mind is on my work that I brought home to do or it is on what work I am anticipating that I must do tomorrow. So this lack of focus means to her that I am not being loving.* He concludes that for Jill, at this particular time, love means giving undivided attention.

Now Jeff asks himself, *Why am I distracted by work? If the work engages so much of my time that I have no time for my wife, then there is too much work. But why would I have too much?* The reasons will vary from person to person. For Jeff, he realizes he has an ongoing desire to feel important, to feel that he is competent and capable. These things feed Jeff's pride. *My job is where I get my sense of accomplishment and worth; there I feel important, competent, and capable. If I do well, colleagues praise me; my boss likes it.* In contrast, Jeff gets little praise at home.

So Jeff's focus is on work, not home. The problem is about emotion, about affection, about feeling good.

We see that the prideful and distorted view of work is keeping Jeff from loving his wife. And it is not that Jeff doesn't love her, nor is it that he does not want to love her. Rather, another emotional drive interferes.

IT IS NOT ENOUGH to view giving
attention as a duty. That perspective
keeps a large part of our heart
(whole self) uninvolved.

We need to let go of our destructive habits. We need to see our compulsions to operate a certain way weakened and diminish. Some of these ways of thinking and habits might have a long history of being defended and justified. They might be harmful but also favorites of ours. As we saw above, some of these might be deeply embedded in things we think we "learned" in the past. Letting them go will involve mourning such perspectives, habits, ingrained motives, attitudes, and patterns.

Let's get back to our example. So if Jeff engages in letting go, then he sees this pattern—this pattern of not giving Jill his full attention—for what it is, namely, a hindrance to love. It is not enough to see this negative pattern as an inconvenience to his wife. It is not enough to view giving attention as a duty and the failure to give attention as the failure of giving a duty. That perspective keeps a large part of Jeff's heart (whole self) uninvolved. That is, of course, an unemotional and distant approach that does not involve his entire self.

Jeff's distractions are hindering love; therefore he should mourn this negative pattern with godly grief. Godly grief leads to repentance (2 Corinthians 7:9–11). If Jeff grieves that negative pattern, then he will work to abandon this harmful way of thinking. In a sense, he needs to gradually subtract something from his life. To reduce the limited emotional pattern he is in, a pattern that may be based on some painful relational history (perhaps his parents only gave love if he "performed" well in school). This pattern is damaging present relationships.

Changing this negative pattern will not happen quickly. When a gardener spreads a weed killer on her lawn, she finds that one application is not enough to get rid of the weeds. She needs to come back over and over again. So likewise in transformation, we need to go back, again and again, detaching ourselves from a habit of harmful patterns of relating, graceless motives, ungodly fears, and prideful attitudes. But as we loosen our strong grip on things, seeing them as more and more repulsive, we will find that old motives will die away like the weeds, and new grass—that is, good affections, proper motivations—will begin to take over.

For Jill and Jeff, it might go like this: They agree that every time Jeff struggles, Jill will say, "You're doing it again." Then Jeff will examine his own heart and ask why he is distracted. He will acknowledge that this motivation is keeping him from showing love and let it go. He must recommit himself to love, not success. Jeff needs to admit, of course, that giving his employer an honest day's work is important. Each of us needs to do all things as to the Lord (Colossians 3:23), including our jobs. But when Jeff recommits himself to love Jill, he is putting Jesus first and foremost. Christ loved, but from the perspective of the world He was not successful.

Jeff concludes, *I will set work aside, listen to my wife* (with a truly engaged listening). For Jill, after their conversation, she will reinforce the behavior by thanking Jeff for his attention.

LETTING CHRISTIAN AFFECTIONS GROW

We all have the capacity for these affections, although our affections may need to be exercised like a muscle. With exercise, our *Christian affections can grow in capacity*. Edwards does not use the term *capacity*, but it is a helpful way to summarize what he says. Having godly affections is not just about having them or not having them; it is also about a growing capacity and a growing desire. He says,

> The more a true saint loves God with a gracious love, the more he desires to love [God], and the more uneasy is he at his want of love to him; the more he hates sin, the more he desires to hate it, and laments that he has so much remaining love to it; the more he mourns for sin, the more he longs to mourn for sin; the more his heart is broke, the more he desires it should be broke; the more he thirsts and longs after God and holiness, the more he longs to long, and breathe out his very soul in longings after God: the kindling and raising of gracious affections

is like kindling a flame; the higher it is raised, the more ardent it is; and the more it burns, the more vehemently does it tend and seek to burn .[8]

Paul speaks in a similar way. In a prayer for the Thessalonians he says, "Now may our God and Father himself, and our Lord Jesus, direct our way to you, and may the Lord make you increase and abound in love for one another and for all, as we do for you" (1 Thessalonians 3:11–12).

And the prayer was gloriously answered, for Paul later says about them that "the love of every one of you for one another is increasing" (2 Thessalonians 1:3). The same is true for the apostle himself. He already loves the Thessalonians. His affectionate language throughout the letters makes that clear (e.g., 1 Thessalonians 2:7–8, 17–19). What is amazing is that he recognizes his own growth in loving them more. But perhaps we should not be surprised. He prayed that the love of the Philippians would grow (Philippians 1:9) and that the hope of the Romans would increase (Romans 15:13).

THE CHALLENGE OF TRANSFORMED AFFECTIONS

Though mentioned before, it bears repeating: we should not expect old perspectives and habits to die a quick death; rather, just the opposite is the case. The transformation of our affections can be hard work.

Why is it such hard work? Often the affections we have and the ways we work in relationships have been learned unconsciously. They have become more gut-level knowledge (implicit knowledge) than intellectual knowledge (explicit knowledge). Explicit knowledge is like my knowledge of the multiplication tables, my anniversary date, or the record overnight low for Chicago (minus 27°F!). I know that I learned these things, I know when I learned them, and I know how I learned them. If Chicago has a colder overnight low, I can simply replace the old figure with a new one. Implicit knowledge is not exactly like that. It has been "learned" in a deep internal place. It has come to us from learning what happened before our earliest memory. It has come to us from our parents' habits that—for good or ill—we accepted as normal. It has come to us by way of habits that we think work, when they actually don't. It has come to us from experiences we had long before we had the intellectual capacity to make sense of the experiences.

Implicit knowledge is like knowing how to ride a bike. When I was almost seven I learned how to do this. It was hard at first; I crashed several times, suffering with aching legs and bloody knees. There were too many things going on at once: watching for traffic or bumps, paying attention to speed and balance, moving the legs, and holding on. Now I think the bike is a great invention. But at first I had to learn balance, rhythm, and how to steer (it's not all about the handlebars; it is partly about leaning). Once learned, the knowledge I have is not conscious, not intellectual, and not explicit. It is not like remembering the date of my anniversary. It is more of a sense and a feel.

Much that happens in our relationships is like that knowledge of how to ride a bike. You have a sense with it, a feel for how it works. It is implicit knowledge. If our parents were sinners—and they were!—then they passed on to us some implicit relational damage.

Please forgive a more personal example. My parents divorced when I was two and then my mom divorced her second husband when I was about seven. Then she was a single parent for almost eight years. My own sinful heart was affected by these experiences; as a result, I developed false views of the world. I was on my own. I needed to take care of myself. There was no one to connect to. Of course, I did not say that to myself. And, of course, I do not believe in my theology that I am on my own, that I need to take care of myself, etc. But that is a perspective ingrained; it comes naturally, even though it might seem contrary to my explicit intellectual belief. It is an implicit, unconsciously learned way of working.

The worst part is that it strikes me as implicitly natural. Abandoning this way of operating is challenging. I cannot unlearn it as easily as I can learn facts. If I have a problem with love, I will not learn to love in a vacuum. I cannot learn to love people while I am in the privacy of my own room reading my Bible and praying to be more loving. Of course, we need to do that. But such an approach is about like saying that I can learn to ride a bike from a book and then expect it all to go well when I first sit on a bike. It won't. I can read of principles from the Bible, valuable ones. But I will need to love by doing it—with all the successes and failures that go with on-the-job training.

WHEN OUR AFFECTIONS are being renewed, our motivations are being renewed [and] we find greater intimacy with God.

But let's not stress the negative. With the hard work comes blessing. When our affections are being renewed, our motivations are being renewed. We find that we are most often motivated to love and obey not out of duty or obligation, but out of longing and joy. As our affections are renewed, we find greater intimacy with God; we enjoy emotional transparency with Him. Even the new deeper grief we feel over sin helps, since we find more motivation to repent.

As our affections are being renewed, day by day, we find that, even though deep pain comes, we have joy more consistently. Lastly, even while enjoying the blessing of life on the old earth, we develop a greater hunger for the new heaven and the new earth, where all transformation will be complete:

> Then I saw a new heaven and a new earth, for the first heaven and the first earth had passed away, and the sea was no more. And I saw the holy city, new Jerusalem, coming down out of heaven from God, prepared as a bride adorned for her husband. And I heard a loud voice from the throne saying, "Behold, the dwelling place of God is with man. He will dwell with them, and they will be his people, and God himself will be with them as their God. He will wipe away every tear from their eyes, and death shall be no more, neither shall there be mourning, nor crying, nor pain anymore, for the former things have passed away. (Revelation 21:1–4)

Questions for Discussion

1. How did you define "transformation" before reading this chapter? How does that definition compare to, or contrast with, the definition given here?
2. In your own words explain *orthodoxy*, *orthopraxy*, and *orthokardia*.
3. Have you noticed that at times your own motivation to be godly comes from hypocrisy? If so, give an example.
4. Why must Christian affections be based on the character of God?
5. The statement "Christian affections are strong not weak" might strike some readers as extreme or threatening. Describe your own reaction.
6. What implicit knowledge do you think you need to unlearn? Explain.
7. Reread Revelation 21:1–4 and give your own reaction.

Suggestions for Further Reading

Edwards, Jonathan. *The Works of Jonathan Edwards, Vol. 2: Religious Affections*. New Haven, Conn.: Yale University Press, 2009.

Leffel, G. Michael. "Emotion and Transformation in the Relational Spirituality Paradigm. Part 1, Prospects and Prescriptions for Reconstructive Dialogue." *Journal of Psychology & Theology* 35 (2007): 263–280.

Notes

Chapter 1: Why Talk about the Emotional Life of a Christian?

1. "Away in a Manger," from stanza 2, source unknown. *The Baptist Hymnal* (Nashville, Convention Press, 1991). The lyrics "Be near me Lord Jesus" are in stanza 3, by John Thomas McFarland. In public domain.

2. Joseph Scriven, "What a Friend We Have in Jesus," *The Baptist Hymnal*. In public domain.

3. Horatio G. Spafford, "It Is Well with My Soul," *The Baptist Hymnal*.

4. D. A. Carson, "Motivations to Appeal to in Our Hearers When We Preach for Conversion," *Themelios* 35, no. 2 (2010): 258–64.

5. A. R. Damasio and G. W. Van Hoesen, "Emotional Disturbances Associated with Focal Lesions of the Limbic Frontal Lobe," in *Neuropsychology of Human Emotion*, ed. K. M. Heilman and P. Satz (New York: Guilford Press, 1983); Patrick Verstichel and Pascale Larrouy, "Drowning Mr. M," *Scientific American Mind* 16, no. 1 (2005): 38–41.

Chapter 2: How Emotions Work

1. For an introduction to the cognitive theory of emotion, see Robert C. Solomon, "Philosophy of Emotion," *Handbook of Emotions*, ed. Michael Lewis, *et al.* (New York: Guilford Press, third edition, 2010), 3–16. For the cognitive theory from a Christian perspective, see chapter 1, "What Is Emotion?" in Matthew A. Elliott, *Faithful Feelings: Rethinking Emotion in the New Testament* (Grand Rapids: Kregel, 2006), 16–55.

2. Those who have been through severe trauma, and those who suffer from bipolar disorder, depression, or other disorders that have a significant biological component, will face special challenges. While there is hope, those readers should enlist professional helpers (physicians, counselors) in the process of emotion change.

3. Robert C. Roberts, *Spiritual Emotions: A Psychology of Christian Virtues* (Grand Rapids: Eerdmans, 2007), 115.

4. For example, see David Matsumoto, *et al.*, "Facial Expressions of Emotion," in *Handbook of Emotions*, ed. Michael Lewis, Jeannette M. Haviland-Jones, and Lisa Feldman Barret, 3rd ed. (New York: Guilford Press, 2010), 211–34.

Chapter 3: The Fruit of the Spirit Is Joy

1. "Joy," at http://dictionary.reference.com/browse/joy.

2. These points are slightly modified from Michael A. Bullmore, "The Four Most Important Biblical Passages for a Christian Environmentalism," *Trinity Journal* NS19 (1998): 143.

3. "Empathy," at http://dictionary.reference.com/browse/empathy.

4. Another key exception exists for professional first responders or caregivers, such as doctors, nurses, therapists, and chaplains, who are required to carefully manage their feelings of empathy lest such feelings prevent or slow needed intervention. For an introduction, see Martin L. Hoffman, "Empathy and Prosocial Behavior," *Oxford Handbook of Philosophy of Emotion*, ed. Peter Goldie (New York: Oxford University Press, 2010), 443–44.

5. Hoffman, "Empathy," 440.

Chapter 5: In My Family, We Never Talked about *Anger*

1. Brian Cox, "Wisconsin Man Gets 25 Years for Road Rage Murder on Edens," *Chicago Tribune*, December 30, 2010. at http://articles.chicagotribune.com/2010-12-30/news/ct-met-road-rage-sentencing-20101230_1_road-rage-murder-road-rage-attack-david-seddon.

2. "Anger, Hostility, and Violent Behavior—Topic Overview" at http://www.webmd.com/balance/tc/anger-and-hostility-topic-overview.

3. Dan Allender and Tremper Longman III, *The Cry of the Soul* (Colorado Springs: NavPress, 1994) 62.

Chapter 6: What If I'm Angry *with* God?

1. John Piper, "Is It Ever Right to Be Angry at God?" October 16, 2002; cited at http://www.desiringgod.org/resource-library/taste-see-articles/is-it-ever-right-to-be-angry-at-god.

2. Ellen Davis Lewin, "Arguing for Authority: A Rhetorical Study of Jeremiah 1:4–19 and 20:7–18," *Journal for the Study of the Old Testament* 32 (1985): 112.

3. Andrew D. Lester, "Why Hast Thou Forsaken Me! Anger at God," *Journal of Pastoral Theology* 16 (2006): 56.

4. Tremper Longman III, "Lament," *Cracking Old Testament Codes: A Guide to Interpreting Literary Genres in the Bible* (Nashville: Broadman & Holman, 1995), 198.

Chapter 7: Is *Love* Only an Action?

1. Rick Warren, "Love Is an Action," from *Daily Scripture Blog*, posted December 20th, 2008, on http://dailyscriptureblog.com/devotional/love-is-an-action.

2. Marvin E. Tate, *Psalms 51-100* (Dallas: Word Books, 1990), 37.

3. Stephen Vorwinde, *Jesus' Emotions in the Gospels* (London: T&T Clark, 2001), 109.

Chapter 8: *Fear*: A Good Kind and A Bad Kind

1. Brian S. Borgman, *Feelings and Faith* (Wheaton: Crossway 2009), 124.

2. Ibid., 128.

3. Because some Greek manuscripts do not contain Luke 22:43–44, some English Bibles might put these verses in brackets or in the margin. See the discussion in Darrell Bock, *Luke 9:51—24:53* (Grand Rapids: Baker Academic, 1996), 1763–64.

4. The word is spelled different ways (*hemathidrosis, hematohidrosis,* and *hematidrosis*). On the phenomenon, see H. R. Jerajani, Bhagyashri Jaju, M. M. Phiske, and Nitin Lade, "Hematohidrosis—A Rare Clinical Phenomenon," *Indian Journal of Dermatology* 54 (2009): 290–92; J. E. Holoubek and A. B. Holoubek, "Blood, Sweat and Fear: A Classification of Hematidrosis," *Journal of Medicine* 27 (1996): 115–33; also William D. Edwards, Wesley J. Gabel, and Floyd E. Hosmer, "On the Physical Death of Jesus Christ," *Journal of the American Medical Association* 255/11 (1986): 1455–1463.

Chapter 9: *Contentment* and *Holy Longing*

1. P. G. Mathew, "Unshakable Christian Contentment," November 22, 2004, at http://www.gracevalley.org/sermon_trans/2004/Unshakable_Christian_Contentment.html.

2. I exclude from consideration uses of the same verb with the meaning "be enough." In these cases the verb has no emotional content. See Matthew 25:9 ("not *enough* oil for us"); John 6:7 ("200 denarii of bread would not *be enough*"); John 14:8 ("show us the Father and it is *enough* for us"); 2 Corinthians 9:8 ("God's grace abounds so that we have *enough* to do every good work"); 2 Corinthians 12:9 ("my grace is *sufficient* for you"). Also, 3 John 10 has a negative use of the same verb ("not *content* with that sin, he refuses the brothers").

Chapter 10: The Loss of *Sadness*

1. Allan V. Horowitz and Jerome C. Wakefield, *The Loss of Sadness* (New York: Oxford Univ. Press, 2007), 29. The title of our chapter comes from the Horowitz and Wakefield book.

2. Robert C. Solomon, *True to Our Feelings* (New York: Oxford Univ. Press, 2007), 72.

3. John Piper, "Palm Sunday: Tears of Sovereign Mercy (Luke 19:28–44)," http://www.desiringgod.org/resource-library/sermons/palm-sunday-tears-of-sovereign-mercy (accessed 5 May 2012).

Chapter 11: Emotions and Spiritual Transformation

1. Here, and in several parts of the discussion, we draw on a three-part series on emotion and transformation entitled "Emotion and Transformation in the Relational Spirituality Paradigm, written by G. Michael Leffel and published in the *Journal of Psychology and Theology* as three articles: Part 1, "Prospects and Prescriptions for Reconstructive Dialogue," 35 (2007), 263–80, here 275; Part 2, "Implicit Morality and 'Minimal Prosociality,'" 281–97; "Part 3, "A Moral Motive Analysis," 298–316.

2. Jonathan Edwards, *A Treatise Concerning Religious Affection* (New York: Cosimo Books, 2009).

3. Ibid., 29.

4. Ibid.

5. Ibid., 176.

6. Ibid., 27.

7. Both comments from Edwards, *Physical Affection*, 347.

8. Ibid., 303.

Acknowledgments

THIS PROJECT WOULD never have gotten started without the encouragement of Parker Hathaway. Parker is the audience development manager of the academic and Bible reference line at Moody Publishers. But two years ago while completing his bachelor's degree at Moody Bible Institute, he took a course on book publishing. One project for the class was to propose a possible book. So one day he just asked me if there was anything I might want to write a book on.

"How about a book on emotion?" I asked. And the rest is history. Thanks, Parker!

Moody Publishers has been easy to work with because of Jim Vincent, my editor. He has shepherded me though the process, while being patient during all my delays and missed deadlines. Thanks, Jim!

In 2011 I had the honor of teaching a year-long class on our emotions to the 11 a.m. Adult Community at my home church, Chain of Lakes Community Bible Church (north of Chicago). Every Sunday morning was filled with discussion, questions, challenges, insights, and clarifications. The class helped me rethink many key passages of Scripture, sharpen my thinking, reword my expression, and relearn what I thought I already knew. Much of their input appears on these pages. Thanks to everyone!

Special thanks goes to Rev. Dr. Bruce Winter, former principal of Queensland Theological College (Australia), who currently serves there as research professor of New Testament. But while I was pursuing graduate work at King's College London in 1990, Bruce was warden of Tyndale House Cambridge (UK). It was there that—one day over tea—he firmly, yet gently and pastorally, let me know that I was pursuing a PhD because I was an emotional cripple. He said I would never really engage in ministry unless I came out of my stoic refuge. That rebuke was painful, but insightful and much needed. Thanks, Bruce!

I tell students at Moody Bible Institute that I have learned more from twenty-eight years of marriage than from seven years of graduate school. While Bruce Winter got me started on the journey toward recovery from stoicism, my wife, Margie, is the one who has been there daily to interact, correct, and encourage. Oh, the stories I could tell! She has been very patient with this slow learner. Thanks, my dear!